A GARDEN • STYLE BOOK

SALAD GARDENS

[SIMPLE SECRETS FOR GLORIOUS GARDENS—INDOORS AND OUT]

MIMI LUEBBERMANN
PHOTOGRAPHY BY FAITH ECHTERMEYER

CHRONICLE BOOKS
SAN FRANCISCO

Library of Congress Cataloging-in-Publication Data available.
ISBN 0-8118-1062-3

Printed in Hong Kong
Cover and interior design by
Aufuldish & Warinner

Distributed in Canada by Raincoast Books,
8680 Cambie Street, Vancouver, B.C. V6P 6M9

10 9 8 7 6 5 4 3 2 1

Chronicle Books
275 Fifth Street
San Francisco, CA 94103

Contents

POTTED SALAD GARDENS TO GROW INDOORS   32

POTTED SALAD GARDENS TO GROW OUTDOORS   40

SALAD GARDENS IN A PATCH OF GROUND   54

INTRODUCTION

Many of us were first introduced to salad gardens through Peter Rabbit, the young scamp who nibbled forbidden lettuces in Beatrix Potter's classic children's book. Mr. McGregor's tidy rows of lettuces and cabbages with accompanying carrots looked so very appealing we all understood why Peter ignored his mother's warning and stole under the garden fence for a quick sampling of both lettuce and danger.

¶ Salads have been a part of humankind's diet for thousands of years. Early foragers picked greens from afar; their descendants transplanted them to their own fields. The ancient Greeks and Romans made lettuces a part of their daily meals and wrote recipes that recommended eating salad greens with a simple vinaigrette of olive oil and vinegar. Medieval herbalists recommended a variety of leaves, like our mesclun salads, to increase digestion, cool the blood, and calm the senses.

¶ Long before vitamin pills, simple salads were considered both medicine and nourishment. Now that it's deemed imperative to eat fresh vegetables for good dietary practice, the kitchen and the medicine cabinet have once again merged. Greens fresh from the garden provide vitamins C and A, calcium, and iron. The dark leafy greens also provide folic acid—essential for healthy pregnancies—and experts tout their high-fiber content as protection against cancer. Our mothers' admonition to "eat your greens because they are good for you" shouldn't prove so difficult to follow if we make our own salad gardens. Besides being nutritious, garden salads have a taste and texture that put the often limp market-purchased varieties to shame.

¶ Many of us started out making salads with the bland but long-lasting, hence convenient, crisphead lettuce (also known as iceberg). The adventure of growing tasty salad gardens begins with educating ourselves on the innumerable variety of salad offerings. To call all leafy salad ingredients "greens" is a misnomer nowadays, for the new dainty lettuces decorate our plates in shades of ruby red and burgundy, as well as chartreuse and forest green. The leaves come in all shapes: some frilly crinolines tipped with burgundy, some deeply cut Matisse oak leaves.

¶ Salad gardens need no longer be dull tasting either. European varieties of leafy vegetables expand your choice of bold new tastes to toss in the salad bowl. Many Asian greens such as mizuna, which enjoy the colder temperatures that butter lettuces abhor, add a spicy taste to salads and can be served wilted or piled up in open-faced sandwiches. Radicchio, a long-beloved Italian specialty, adds a tangy bitterness to mixed salads and combines exceptionally with apples and pears for a chic, updated Waldorf. The mesclun mixes add a new dimension to salad gardening, with as many as ten different types of lettuce all grown and harvested together.

¶ Salad greens that grow in straight rows across acres of ground grow just as tidily in pocket gardens, rooftop containers, and outdoor windowsills. Making a salad garden can be as easy as seeding a salad bowl–sized container on your back porch or on an outdoor landing that receives about four hours of sun a day. If you have a small city garden, a tiny plot sown successively can produce garden-fresh salads all season long. Consider tucking baby lettuces into vegetable beds between slow-growing corn or beans; they'll enjoy the shade during high summer and be ready for harvest before the larger plants squeeze

them out. Container-grown lettuces can decorate decks and porches while providing crisp dinner salads just a step away from the kitchen.

¶ Concentrate for a moment solely on the colors and shapes of salad greens, and you'll be able to see them planted in many areas of the garden. Their jewel-like colors decorate the garden as beautifully as the salad plate. Add red lettuces or swirls of curly escarole as color and texture accents between flowers in a container or flower bed. In mild climates the edible ornamental kale makes a winter vegetable bed in fall and winter as colorful as a July flower border. Or edge your garden beds with nasturtiums for neon-bright edible flowers and a peppery salad leaf.

¶ Many other ingredients besides greens go into making a great salad. Herbs, those flavor power-blasts, can be year-round garden residents, planted either in a container if you need to bring them inside during winter or directly in the ground in mild-winter areas. Their leaves flavor oils, vinegars, and raw greens, and their flowers spot salads with lively colors. Alliums, from chives to garlic and onions, add an unmistakable flavor many cooks insist absolutely makes a salad. Sprouts grown on windowsills can be a salad in and of themselves, or you can add their crunchy texture to any lettuce mix. Beyond green salad gardens and the scope of this book is a whole world of vegetables, from tomatoes to cooked potatoes, that can gussy up a leafy salad.

¶ A salad garden can be kept full almost all year-round in most areas. There are winter-hardy lettuce varieties that don't mind a touch of cold; if frosts are light and you protect the lettuce beds under a south-facing overhang, they'll supply your household all winter long. Special plastic hoops or greenhouse cloth also protect tender greens from cool nights or late-fall or spring frosts. The hardy kale, like Garrison Keillor's Minnesotans, prefers winter's chill, which improves its flavor. Greens for early spring can be started in flats inside the house or greenhouse to mature quickly in the spring-cool garden soil. Successive sowings through spring and summer will provide salad bowls of greens into the late autumn. In even the hottest climates, there are cool, partially shaded spots to grow lettuces.

¶ From my childhood, I remember with fondness neat wedges of iceberg lettuce dolloped with pickle-dotted dressing, the traditional salad served at restaurants. I loved neatly slicing off bits, working my way toward an empty plate. When I stayed one summer with my aunt and uncle in England, we kids were sent to pick the luncheon salad out of the garden every Sunday. There was no iceberg in sight. The lovely leaves my cousins showed me how to harvest expanded my view of just what a salad might be.

¶ As a new gardener, I began growing lettuces in containers, for I had little garden space and an army of voracious snails and slugs. This method provided a generous harvest and kept the pests at bay. With four medium-sized containers, one replanted every month or so with different types of lettuce, I had enough greens for salads and sandwiches and plenty of almost-country relaxation when I went out harvesting before the meal.

¶ Every winter's end, I have an overwhelming craving, a kind of primal, post-hibernation instinct—which I happily indulge—to eat quantities of greens. My body aches for baby leaves of kale dressed with a hot bacon-bits vinaigrette, tender little lettuces tossed with lemon oil and a drop of balsamic vinegar, or Asian greens mixed with a sesame oil vinaigrette. My passion for greens has drawn me to experiment with salad greens in nonsectarian salad ways. I sauté lettuce in a pearl of butter, toss it with a thimble of cream, and serve it up as a warm vegetable. Raddichio is halved and baked under a blanket of bread crumbs in puddles of garlicky olive oil. Fresh tender kale is chopped, steamed, tossed with sage, salt, and pepper, and baked as stuffing in a whole chicken. Salad greens are multitalented vegetables.

¶ Of course, tossing your stalwart greens the traditional way with just a bit of good olive oil, a hint of vinegar, and a soupçon of garlic provides the simplest, most elegant salad. Although you can load up your salads like the impressive display of a salad bar, adding cucumbers, tomatoes, poached asparagus, or even peppered melon, fresh greens on their own are always enough. Strolling out to snip off the salad leaves and a few herbs for a moment-fresh salad brings proprietary pleasure: You know that you have raised healthy, nutritious food that you can pick at its peak of flavor for your friends' greatest dining satisfaction.

CHARACTERISTICS OF SALAD GREENS

We owe homage to the commercial salad bar for expanding our concept of a salad beyond squares of iceberg lettuce sprinkled with shreds of carrot and ornamented with two cherry tomatoes and a sprig of parsley. It was the glittering array of lettuce, spinach, thin-sliced purple cabbage, green onions, plus a hundred accoutrements from corn to mushrooms to pickles that first gave us the freedom to reassess the lively potential of our daily salad.

¶ Today's salad has rocketed beyond even the salad bar offerings. A diner may order up a house salad and barely recognize the different leaves that fill the plate. Salad greens available as seeds and nursery-grown starts for the home gardener come in a range almost beyond definition in its delicious variety.

¶ The reintroduction of old-fashioned hot dressings that just wilt the greens opens the gate to still more choices of salad plants. The bold-tasting young leaves of the *Brassicas* and hardy kales are toned down by a warm dressing. Even peppery Asian mustards find a place in salads when picked young and tossed with sesame oil, a dash of soy sauce, and fresh lemon juice. Besides these high-toned salad ingredients, a number of old-fashioned weeds foraged by our ancestors have come back into grace. Flavorful arugula and mache have made a delicious reentry into the salad bowl.

¶ Botanically, most of our salad greens come from the Compositae, or daisy, family, which includes asters, sunflowers, and all the lettuces. The leafy *Brassicas* such as cabbage, both western and Asian, are from the Cruciferae family. Salad greens are not a distinct group in terms of their growing requirements. Some are frost hardy, some not. They have different growing seasons and need various amounts of light and heat. What salad greens have in common is delicate, succulent leaves—albeit sometimes with a hint of bitterness or a peppery bite.

¶ When laying out your salad garden, plan for the different growing styles of your greens. Cos lettuces, the romaine varieties, form tall columns of lettuces, so they can be more tightly spaced than head, or cabbage, lettuces, which grow in round clumps. Space cos lettuces 6 inches apart with 6 inches between rows. Space head lettuces 8 inches apart with 8 inches between rows. Cos and head lettuce are usually grown to maturity and the whole head harvested at once.

¶ The loose-leaf lettuces provide an extended harvest, for you keep picking the outer leaves of each plant as you need, until the plant ends the growing period by going to seed. You can grow loose-leaf lettuces easily in containers or if you wish in rows, but the most space-efficient way is to thickly sow them in cut-and-come-again beds, sprinkling the seeds evenly over the bed so that it becomes totally covered with plants. To harvest, trim a section of the bed down to the plant crowns and leave them to regrow new leaves, which you can harvest several weeks later in the same manner.

¶ Salad greens are mostly annual plants that sprout and grow to maturity in one growing season. Some greens, such as the lemony flavored sorrel, are perennials; they grow to maturity in one season, you harvest some of the leaves, and the plants keep growing year after year. The intensely flavored Italian flat-leaf parsley, curly parsley, and kale are biennials; they like to start growing in the summer season, continue to grow throughout the

winter, and then if left unharvested come to flower early the next summer.

¶ Salad greens differ in the amount of cold and heat they can tolerate. Some greens, such as arugula and the Asian mustards, grow best during cool spring and fall weather; others, such as kale, develop their flavor after a touch of frost. Some lettuces are winter-hardy in mild climates, surviving light frosts, although their leaves may be thicker and a bit tougher than those of summer varieties. Many, but not all, salad greens abhor intense summer heat, for it makes them grow flower stalks, and the leaves become bitter and inedible. Choose varieties of salad greens that match your growing season and climate.

¶ Salad greens share the characteristic of succulent leaves, but their tastes are quite distinct. Mrs. Beaton, writing in 1861, described lettuce as "having a bland and pellucid juice, with little taste or smell, and having a cooling and soothing influence on the system." *Lactuca sativa* is in fact named for its milky white sap. The taste of lettuces is milder than that of many other salad greens.

¶ Some salad greens are distinctly sassy. The mustards of the *Brassica* group tingle the tongue with a zip that becomes more pronounced the older the plant and the warmer the weather. In mild climates many of the mustards grow all winter long, surviving light frosts and heavy rains to provide salads in the coldest months. Asian greens have a strong taste that can stand up to full-flavored salad dressings. Harvest them for salad when the leaves are still small and tender. Cress gives a sharp, peppery bite to the taste buds. It grows quickly; harvest the pale sprouts or leave them until they're green.

¶ Kale, both the decorative type and the garden variety, likes to grow in cool weather. As it matures, the leaves become too tough for raw salads, but try them as the base of a wilted salad, or just quickly sauté them in a hot salad dressing for a warm salad on a cold evening. Kale provides great quantities of folic acid, an essential ingredient in our diet not easily found in other foods. Recent studies have shown that folic acid is critical for healthy pregnancies.

¶ Salad greens have a tendency to bolt in warm weather: The leaves harden and become bitter, a flower stalk grows up from the center of the plant and produces seeds. Planting late in the spring increases the risk of bolting, but an early bout of summer heat may cause even early spring sowings to rush to finish their growth cycle. Many gardeners prefer to eat their greens as small baby greens, beginning to harvest the outer leaves as soon as the plants reach 3 or so inches high. This ensures a good harvest before the greens have a chance to bolt.

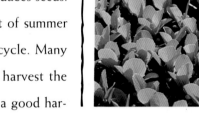

¶ Newly available are seed packets of mixed greens, sometimes named mesclun. Mesclun provides a delicious salad bowl mix, often ten or more different varieties of greens. All are loose-leaf varieties so sow the seeds in cut-and-come-again beds or in rows, harvesting outer leaves of the plants as they grow.

¶ We often think of salads as temporary residents in our warm-weather gardens, but in truth, many perennials and herbs suitable for inclusion in the salad bowl overwinter outdoors successfully, providing salad ingredients year after year. Gardeners in cold-winter areas can either pot them up out of the ground in fall, or simply container-raise them from infancy.

¶ Nurseries and seed catalogues are providing a greater selection of salad greens every year. Don't forget to experiment with a couple of different types every season, and keep a garden diary of what you have planted, when you planted, and how your harvest turns out.

About growing salad greens

Salad greens grow best when provided with water, nutrients, adequate light, and healthy, friable soil. To keep the leaves succulent and tender, the plants need to grow quickly. Understanding how a plant grows and how you can create an environment that stimulates healthy growth will take some of the mystery out of gardening. A few need a certain temperature range, which makes them better suited to growing in particular seasons or climates. Most lettuces prefer cooler seasons, although not too cool: Nippy temperatures will produce frost bite on some types. There are some varieties that hold out against hot weather, continuing to grow over a long season without bolting. In mild-winter areas with only light frosts, cold-tolerant greens can be kept growing in the garden all winter long. A greenhouse provides the cold-winter gardener with a continued harvest even when the ground outside is covered with snow.

Water

Water carries nutrients from the soil up through the roots and stem to the leaves. As it evaporates through pores in the leaves, the roots draw more water from the soil, like straws sucking up liquid.

¶ During periods of high evaporation, such as hot or windy days, the rate of water loss from the leaves increases, so the roots need more water. When the leaves lose more water than the roots can quickly replenish, the plant wilts. A properly watered plant is one that has constant access to readily available water in the soil. During hot and windy days, make sure to increase your watering.

¶ Soil composition affects the amount of water available for plants and the health of their roots. Very sandy soil drains quickly, so plants have less water available; clay soils drain less readily but may not be good for plant roots. The air in the spaces between soil particles contains the same gases as our atmosphere; the roots need the oxygen to breathe. When soil is filled with water, oxygen is pushed out and consequently is not available to the roots. Just as plants can die from too little water, they can die from too much. Normally when an area of soil fills with water, gravity pulls the water down through the spaces between the soil particles, allowing oxygen to fill them again.  Certain factors, such as heavy clay soils, the lack of a hole in a planting container, or a layer of rocks at the bottom of a planting container, prevent proper drainage and plant roots suffocate. Even though it is traditional to add rocks or crockery to the bottom of containers, they often dam the flow of drainage water, so ignore that century-old instruction and just fill the container with potting soil.

¶ Adding plenty of organic matter to your garden beds before you plant is an excellent way to improve soil composition. In sandy soils the organic matter retains moisture; compost absorbs water like a sponge, then holds it available for the plant roots. In clay soils the compost breaks up the clay particles, creating spaces through which water can drain and oxygen can refill. Use your own homemade compost, or purchase aged compost to dig into the soil.

SOILS AND POTTING MIXES

Soil is a mixture of three particles—sand, silt, and clay—plus any organic matter. The silt, clay, and organic matter interact with soil water and provide nutrients to the plant roots. Sand, although chemically inert, also plays an important role in plant health. The largest in size of the particles, sand creates correspondingly large spaces between the soil particles, which contributes to fast drainage, high oxygen concentrations, and good vertical water movement.

¶ The organic matter in soils is mostly old plant material decomposing under constant attack by bacteria and fungi, which over time liberate mineral elements that are essential to plants for their growth. The bacteria and fungi also benefit plants by fighting off microorganisms that cause plant diseases.

¶ A good garden soil crumbles easily in your hand. You may have seen die-hard gardeners or farmers sniffing the soil; they are checking its quality. Healthy soil has a rich earthy smell because of its organic material. Your soil should have this good smell, and you should see small bits of decomposed compost among the grains of soil when you look closely. Your spade should slide into the ground easily, and water in a planting hole should drain out slowly but steadily. Good soil produces good plants, so if your plants are not growing well and you do not see signs of disease or insect problems, check with your local nursery for a location to have your soil tested.

¶ For container plantings, use a good-quality potting mix to ensure it retains moisture, drains well, and does not become concrete-hard in late summer. Commercial potting mixes have been sterilized, which make them cleaner than decomposing materials for growing plants indoors.

PREPARING THE GARDEN BED

For garden beds, prepare the soil two to three weeks before your seeds or transplants will be ready to set out. If the soil is so wet that it falls off the shovel in clumps, you will have to wait to get started until the soil dries some or risk compacting the ground, making it rock hard. Compacted soil has less oxygen so the roots suffer from oxygen deprivation and your plants will not grow successfully.

¶ First remove existing plant material such as weeds or plants that you no longer want to grow there. Add 4 inches of organic compost and with a shovel, a spade, or a machine such as a Rototiller, turn over the soil to a depth of 12 to 18 inches. Water the turned soil and allow any undesirable seeds that may be in the ground to sprout. When the ground is damp but not soggy, remove the unwanted plant material once again. Using a hoe or shovel, break up any clods and rake the surface smooth for planting.

FERTILIZERS AND pH BALANCE

The major nutrients needed for plant growth are nitrogen, phosphorus, and potassium (N, P, and K). A plant removes these nutrients from the soil and uses them to grow. Adding fertilizer to the soil replaces the missing or used-up nutrients, allowing the plant to continue its growth. Because nutrient needs are greatest during periods of rapid growth, fertilize your lettuce beds when you are preparing them for planting. That way, the new plants will have fertilizer available to them.

¶ Commercial fertilizers list their contents as the percentage of each nutrient, in the order nitrogen-phosphorus-potassium. For example, an NPK formula of 10-10-10 has equal amounts of nitrogen, phosphorus, and potassium. You may want to consider using organic fertilizers in your vegetable garden. Choose the new brands with NPK formulas, or use a combination of bonemeal, bloodmeal, wood ashes, and fish emulsion to build up the fertility of your soil. Some gardeners prefer the new slow-release granulated organic fertilizers they add before planting to the liquid fertilizers that need to be applied twice a month. Try the different methods to find one that works best for you. Although there have been no conclusive studies, there are a number of testimonials to the improved taste of vegetables that are organically grown.

¶ Plant growth also depends upon soil chemistry. The pH (potential hydrogen) balance of the soil affects how well a plant absorbs nutrients from the soil. Acid soils have a pH of 6.9 and lower; alkaline soils have a pH of 7.1 and higher. Check with your local nursery to find the special products to test your pH level, and then add appropriate amendments to improve the pH of your soil. Most salad greens prefer a slightly acid soil.

¶ Salad greens growing in containers need regular fertilizing because there is only a limited volume of soil for their roots and regular watering leaches out the nutrients. Apply a liquid fertilizer every two weeks.

STARTING FROM SEEDS

Starting your own salad greens from seeds is easy, and it offers you the advantage of growing a wide range of varieties that nurseries do not regularly stock as small plants. If you live in a cold climate with a short growing season, starting seeds inside produces vigorous plants that are ready for transplanting when the ground warms up. Seeds also can be sown directly into the ground later, after the warmth of spring has brought the ground temperature up to a level that encourages germination. Whether you plan to sow indoors or outdoors, order your seeds for spring and summer sowing in January to make sure you start with fresh high-quality stock. (Some seed sources are listed on pages 103–4.)

¶ Check at your nursery for the choice of seed starting kits, such as Styrofoam flats, plastic six-packs, or peat pots. Choose pots or containers with individual sections for each seedling so that the transplants will pop out of them easily.

¶ Seeds need temperatures between 65° and 75°F to germinate. Some gardeners place heat mats underneath germinating trays to keep the soil evenly warm. A sunny south window may provide enough warmth and light. If not, you can hang Gro-lights or full-spectrum lights 4 to 6 inches above the containers. If your plants lean toward the light source and look skinny and weak, they are not getting enough light.

¶ Start your seeds six to eight weeks before you want to put plants outside into the ground or into containers. You can buy potting mix or you can make your own with equal quantities of vermiculite, perlite, and peat moss. It is important to use a sterilized mix to avoid diseases that infect seedlings. To make sure the plants get off to a good start, add an all-purpose fertilizer to the mix according to the directions on the fertilizer container or once the seedlings are 1 inch high, water them once a week with a low-nitrogen fertilizer diluted to half strength.

¶ Thoroughly moisten the mix with water, then fill the seed container to within 1 inch of the rim. Check the recommended directions on the seed packet to sow the seeds at the correct depth and spacing. After you have sown the seeds, pat down the mix firmly and water carefully so you don't dislodge the seeds. Keep the mix moist but not soggy to avoid encouraging fungal infections. Place the seed containers where they get two to four hours of bright sun a day. If the seedlings begin to stretch up, lean over, and look leggy, they are not receiving enough light. When roots begin to show at the bottom of the container, the young plants are ready to be set out of doors or into larger containers. You do not want your plants to become potbound as this can retard their growth.

TRANSPLANTING YOUNG PLANTS

Because young plants raised indoors or in a greenhouse are tender, you need to accustom them to the more variable temperatures outdoors before you set them into the garden. This process is called hardening off. For one week before you plant them, set the young plants outdoors during the day only. Keep them in the shade at first and then gradually move them into the sun. When you plant them, do it in the late afternoon, to lessen the stress caused by the heat of the day.

¶ To transplant, gently tap out the little plant from its container, taking care to keep the root ball and all its potting mix intact. Check the required spacing for the plants. Make sure to leave enough room so plants do not become crowded as they mature. Make a hole in the planting bed and set in the plant so the top of the root ball is level with the soil. Tamp down the soil firmly around the root ball, making sure the plant is set securely into the ground. Water well.

Cut-and-Come-Again Sowing

The seeds of mesclun lettuce mixes and loose-leaf lettuces as well as other salad greens such as Asian mustards and kale can be sown in containers or beds so thickly that they form a carpet of delectable greens. As the plants mature, keep thinning them for platters of baby greens. Or snip or cut off the leaves right back to within 1 inch of the ground. The crowns will sprout new leaves for a second harvest.

Interplanting

Because most lettuces grow quickly and don't mind a little shade as they mature, you can tuck them between slower-growing plants. Interplanting lettuces between baby squash at the beginning of the spring planting season guarantees you a harvest of lettuces before the squash become so big they squeeze them out. In hot-summer climates, look for spaces that will provide some light shade for the lettuces—underneath sunflowers or between rows of bush beans or widely planted corn. Don't forget that lettuces add texture and color to the flower border. Consider interplanting lettuces between flowering annuals or among the fading foliage from a spring bulb display.

Planting Container Plants

Salad greens grow successfully in containers, making them perfect for gardens on fire escapes, small balconies, or even rooftops. Keeping containers watered evenly is one of the most difficult jobs in container gardening. A potting mix formulated for containers holds water better than regular compost formulated as an amendment for garden soil.

A drip system will help regulate watering, but if that is not possible, try to water your containers on a regular schedule. If the weather becomes windy or hot, increase your watering and use a fine mister at least once a day on the leaves of the plants. Check the soil dampness by poking a finger down at least 2 inches into the soil every week. Plastic containers retain moisture longer than unglazed ceramic or pottery containers.

SUCCESSIVE PLANTINGS

Many gardeners with limited vegetable garden space plant successively to squeeze in as many months of harvest as possible. While plants are starting to mature in garden beds, savvy gardeners start new seeds in trays, so that as soon as they finish harvesting one crop of greens, there are baby-size new transplants ready to set in the garden. One can also alternate two sections of the garden, starting one while harvesting the other. Successive planting means you never have a garden bed empty, so your salad bowl is always full.

FROST PROTECTION

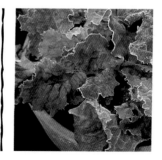

Hardy and *tender* are two words tossed around by gardeners to roughly distinguish how well a plant withstands cold. Tender plants do not like cold temperatures, and a freeze may kill them. Hardy plants stand up to a certain amount of cold and are often described as hardy to a certain temperature—for example, "hardy to 32°F." Half-hardy plants will usually survive a cold spell, but may not survive extended cold weather.

¶ Lettuces are the most tender salad green. Plant your fall-crop or early spring lettuces in the most protected spots in your garden. South-facing walls stay relatively warm because they absorb the winter sun. Plants sequestered at their base, or even better, under a south-facing roof line of a building, are usually in the warmest spot in the garden. Mulch your lettuces heavily just before the frost season begins, or purchase some plastic or frost-resistant covering to make temporary greenhouses for an extended growing season.

¶ If you have a mild winter and want to extend your harvest, try planting kale and winter-tough lettuce varieties like 'Winter Density'. Catalogues always mention the salad greens that can stand up to frosts, so try planting these types to keep fresh greens on your table in the cold months.

PESTS AND DISEASES

Salad greens beckon delectably to quantities of different creatures that compete with the gardener for a share of the succulent delicacies. Yet knowing your greens are destined for your plate must make you cautious about the means you use to protect your harvest. Try the new series of organic soap-based pesticides that suffocate pests with fatty acids harmless to people and animals. Look into some of the biological controls, such as lacewings and trichogramma wasps (very tiny and not like their larger annoying relatives), which attack plant pests without bothering you. Consider using bacillus thuringiensis (BT), a bacteria spray that kills caterpillars without leaving any harmful residue for humans. Although protecting your harvest by organic methods may be more labor intensive, the production of safe and nutritious greens for yourself and your family is a clear incentive.

¶ In moist climates, slugs and snails can become very persistent in the spring or fall. Look for bait specially formulated for vegetable garden use and put it out in small containers such as empty juice cans. Alternatively, maintain a vigilant watch, going out in the evening with a flashlight to handpick the slugs and snails into a bag and discard it, tightly tied, into the garbage.

¶ Earwigs love to perforate lettuce leaves with dainty and not so dainty holes. Roll up a newspaper loosely and leave it in the salad garden. In the morning, shake out the earwigs and destroy them. It may take several nights for your earwig colony to choose the newspaper hotel, but persevere.

¶ Viruses and fungi also attack salad greens, creating stunted, sometimes unusually colored plants. As soon as you notice any infected plants, make sure to pull them out and discard them into the garbage. The best protection against soilborne fungal diseases comes from digging in generous quantities of organic compost that encourages beneficial microbes. If soilborne diseases persist in your garden, consider growing salad greens in containers or raised planter beds filled with sterile soil.

¶ As you become confident in your planning and planting of salad greens, make sure not to fall into a rut. Experiment with different varieties of salad greens in different locations in your garden. Keep a garden diary and every year try some of the new varieties of salad greens introduced by seed companies and nurseries.

POTTED
SALAD
GARDENS
TO GROW
INDOORS

rowing salad gardens indoors may, at first thought, seem impossible. But gardeners have long loved a challenge. Many different reasons account for the at-first-glance unreasonable desire to convert your sunny kitchen windowsills into a garden. Short winter days with their attendant long nights make growing greens outside impossible for all but those lucky gardeners who live in mild-winter climates. Still, the gardening urge doesn't die because of uncooperative weather. It is as though a gauntlet has been cast down. Try growing a few indoor salad ingredients to add a homegrown flavor to winter salads of purchased greens. Even in the midst of spring's abundance, sprouts add a different dimension to salads, making the kitchen window a useful adjunct of the garden.

Crunchy seed sprouts are just the thing to vary the usual texture of lettuce leaves and to put a new zip into sandwiches. The fast-growing cress needs to be sown successively for continued pleasure. The mustards make great additions to your salads and to anything from sandwiches to cooked vegetables or soups—sprinkle them over the top much as you used parsley in the olden days. Try adding some herbs to your sunny windowsill during the winter months to spice up your salads. Find as bright and sunny a location as you have available, and make sure to water the plants regularly and nourish them once a month with an organic fertilizer. Once warm spring days have returned, you can place the containers of herbs outside. The convenience and pleasure of snipping a few herbs to toss in your salads may convert you to maintaining a few containers inside all year long.

SPROUTED SEED HARVEST

Sprouts make fine lettuce substitutes the year around, providing greens even in the coldest winter months. Try growing sprouts right next to the kitchen sink, where you'll see them and remember to water them. Use them in an exclusively fresh sprout salad, in leafy salads as a textural surprise, or on sandwiches to replace lettuce. Be sure to experiment with different types of sprouts to find the flavors and textures you prefer. Of course, avoid buying seed treated with chemicals. ¶ **HOW TO DO IT** ¶ Use a clean quart canning jar with a metal lid and screw-on seal. Cut a piece of cheesecloth or hardware cloth slightly larger than the metal lid. Store the metal lid; you don't need it for growing sprouts. Add the seeds to the bottom of the jar, place the circle of cloth over the top, and screw it down tightly as you would the regular lid. The cloth screen should be taut across the mouth of the jar. Pour water through the screen to cover the sprout seeds. After one or two hours, turn the jar over and drain out the water. Rinse the seeds and sprouts this way once or twice a day so that they stay moist. ¶ When the sprouts are 2 or 3 inches tall, remove the screen, rinse, and drain. Use the sprouts immediately or store them in a plastic bag in the refrigerator for up to three days. ¶ Screens made of hardware cloth may be reused but a fresh piece of cheesecloth must be cut for each batch of seeds.

Wheatberry Sprouts
Triticum aestivum

❧

Radish Sprouts
Raphanus sativus

❧

Onion Sprouts
Allium sativum

❧

Alfalfa Sprouts
Medicago sativa

❧

Sunflower Sprouts
Helianthus annuus

❧

What You Need
Seeds
1 quart canning jar with screw-on lid
Hardware cloth or cheesecloth

❧

Recommended Varieties
Any available

❧

Growing Conditions
Bright spot on a counter

❧

Hardiness
Tender

❧

When to Buy
Anytime

❧

When to Sow
Anytime

❧

When to Harvest
When 2 to 3 inches tall

❧

CRESS WINDOWSILL GARDEN

Cress grows like the dickens, shooting out of the ground eager to reach maturity, somewhat like teenagers. Its peppery flavor teams up nicely with mild lettuces, or you can use it as an herbal condiment, chopping and sprinkling it over vegetables, like parsley. Cress grows indoors on a sunny windowsill, but keep it happily watered. Its little green shoots are ready for harvest when they are quite tiny. You may want to keep several containers going, one just starting and one ready for harvest so you never run out. Grow your cress in pretty rectangular containers, or if you wish, sprout cress in your sprouts jar (page 35). ¶ **HOW TO DO IT** ¶ Fill the container with potting mix to within 1 inch of the rim. Water the mix until it is thoroughly moist. Gently sprinkle seeds over the surface of the mix in a thick layer. Cover the seeds with ¼ inch of potting mix. Pat down the surface and water lightly. Place the container on a counter or windowsill where it will receive bright light, and keep the soil moist but not soggy.

Cress, Peppergrass
Lepidium sativum

What You Need
1 packet of seeds
1 container 10 inches in diameter and
4 inches deep
Potting mix

Recommended Varieties
Curly cress or peppergrass

Growing Conditions
Bright light

Hardiness
Tender

When to Buy
Anytime

When to Sow
Anytime

When to Harvest
After 10 days or when seedlings are
2 inches high

MUSTARD SNIPPING GARDEN

Mustards will grow well indoors for a harvest of baby greens to add to your salad plate. As mature plants, the leaves can sting, but ¼-inch leaves have a delicious taste and just a hint of bite. Grow several containers and alternate harvesting them in a cut-and-come-again snipping fashion so you can reap at least three harvests a container. ¶ **HOW TO DO IT** ¶ Fill the container with potting mix to within 1 inch of the rim. Water the mix until it is thoroughly moist. Gently sprinkle seeds over the surface of the mix in a thick layer. Cover the seeds with ¼ inch of potting mix. Pat down the surface and water lightly. Place the container on a counter or windowsill where it will receive bright light, and keep the soil moist but not soggy.

Assorted Mustards
Brassicaceae
⁂

What You Need
1 packet of seeds
1 container 10 inches in diameter and
4 inches deep
Potting mix
⁂

Recommended Varieties
Red mustard, mizuna
⁂

Growing Conditions
Bright light
⁂

Hardiness
Tender
⁂

When to Buy
All year long
⁂

When to Sow
Anytime
⁂

When to Harvest
After 14 days or when seedlings
are 1 inch high
⁂

POTTED SALAD GARDENS TO GROW OUTDOORS

Though we love the look in glossy photographs of lettuce beds stretching to the horizon line, in truth most of us live contentedly on small city lots. Indeed, back gardens in the city may be

fire escapes or balconies that receive sunlight only a precious few hours a day. Lettuces, with their comparatively shallow root systems, grow very well in small containers. If you have the room for larger containers, your harvest will be abundant. Container gardening expands your garden space because you can put to use driveways, decks, outdoor stairways, rooftops, and window boxes. Look around for an area convenient to water and with about three or four hours of sunlight a day, or dappled sunshine in the summer. Baking afternoon sun may be too hot for some summer greens grown in containers. ❧ Part of the pleasure of container gardening comes from the delight of organizing and arranging your collection aesthetically, in the same way a connoisseur of antique porcelain fusses to show off the finest pieces in an elaborate plan of heights, colors, and lighting. Think of your container collection as a storefront. Plant your greens in different pots, at different heights, and fill them to overflowing with sparkling edible flowers and a hunger-satisfying mix of greens, herbs, and onions. Playing with colors, textures, and shapes can be a reflective and meditative exercise. Walking out to cut lettuce should bring a lifting of your heart, as well as the pleasure of filling the salad bowl to the very brim. ❧ Make sure to place your container garden near your kitchen, for ready access to your homegrown bounty. ❧ The tricky parts of container gardening are planning a steady, successive supply of greens and making sure your containers stay well watered. Plan on sowing seeds every six weeks to keep your harvest going, and make sure to set up a regular watering and fertilizing schedule.

Bouquet of red salad greens

Container gardeners with limited growing space and a desire to grow salads sometimes feel they must sacrifice aesthetics for the mundane practicality of crop raising. Not so. The red lettuces are beautiful in their leaf color and a presentation of them perks up the diner's plate at any table. Although described as red in all the seed catalogues, in truth their color approximates more of a deep reddish-bronzy tone, and sometimes the color seems just brushed on over the green leaves. ¶ The red leaves look spectacular growing in green or blue containers. Experiment with growing the brightly colored leaves in arrangements of contrasting colored containers. Some varieties are quite cold hardy. ¶ **HOW TO DO IT** ¶ In spring, after the last chance of frost, you can safely plant your lettuces. When the plants have two sets of true leaves they are ready to set out in containers. Harden them off for a week by leaving them outside in a protected area during the day and bringing them inside at night. Before planting, submerge the transplants in their containers in a sink or bucket of water until air bubbles cease to appear. ¶ Fill each container with potting mix to within 2 inches of the rim. Water the mix until it is thoroughly moist. Space the plants evenly in the containers, about 2 to 4 inches apart. Scoop out holes large enough for the roots of the plants. Gently remove each lettuce plant and its potting mix from its container and plant it so that the root ball is level with the surface of the mix. Fill the hole with mix, packing it gently around the roots. Pat down the surface and water to fill in any air pockets. ¶ Mulch plants with organic compost spread 1 inch deep. Place the containers where they will receive four hours of sun a day. Keep the soil moist but not soggy. Fertilize every two weeks with a liquid fertilizer diluted to half strength.

Red Lettuces
Lactuca sativa

What You Need
12 lettuce plants
4 containers 10 inches in diameter and 12 inches deep
Potting mix
Organic compost
Liquid organic fertilizer

Recommended Varieties
'Red Oak Leaf', 'Red Lollo', 'Rossimo', 'Deer Tongue'

Cold Hardy Types
'Brune d'Hiver', 'Rouge d'Hiver', 'Red Montpelier', or 'Rougette du Midi'

Growing Conditions
4 hours of direct sun

Hardiness
Tender, protect from frosts

When to Buy
From spring to late summer from nurseries or specialty garden shops

When to Plant
After the last frost

When to Harvest
When outer leaves are 3 to 5 inches long

CHILD'S SALAD GARDEN

When children grow their own salads, they eat them with the relish and delight of ownership. A small container near the kitchen door makes watching, watering, and harvesting convenient for both child and parent. Of course, you may need to do a little secretive midnight watering, for children have a hard time keeping containers adequately watered. To make success more instantaneous, start with small lettuce plants rather than seeds. The radishes must be sown directly in the container, for root crops do not transplant successfully, but they grow so hurriedly, they'll catch up with the lettuce. ¶ Start a May Day tradition of presenting a container, potting mix, and a selection of seeds to a child you know. If you can also find a miniature whisk, the child will be thrilled to whip up the salad dressing. ¶ **HOW TO DO IT** ¶ In spring, after the last chance of frost, you can safely plant your lettuces. When the plants have two sets of true leaves they are ready to plant in the container. Harden them off for a week by leaving them outside in a protected area during the day and bringing them inside at night. Before planting, submerge the transplants in their containers in a sink or bucket of water until air bubbles cease to appear. ¶ Fill the container with potting mix to within 2 inches of the rim. Water the mix until it is thoroughly moist. Space the lettuces evenly in the container, about 2 to 4 inches apart. Scoop out holes large enough for the roots of the lettuce plants. Gently remove each lettuce plant and its potting mix from its container, and plant it so that the root ball is level with the surface of the mix. Fill the hole with mix, packing it gently around the roots. Pat down the surface and water lightly to fill in any air pockets. Push a radish seed ¹/₄ inch down into the mix between each plant. ¶ Place the container where it will receive four hours of sun a day, and keep the soil moist but not soggy. Fertilize every two weeks with a liquid fertilizer diluted to half strength. ¶ If you are seeding the lettuce directly into the container, follow the directions for direct seeding on pages 25–7.

Lettuces
Lactuca sativa
❧

Radishes
Raphanus sativus
❧

What You Need
6 lettuce plants
1 packet of radish seeds
1 container 20 inches in diameter and
10 inches deep
Potting mix
Liquid organic fertilizer
❧

Recommended Varieties
Lettuce: 'Tom Thumb', 'Lovina', 'Red
Sails', 'Oak Leaf'
Radish: 'Flamboyant', 'Easter Egg'
❧

Growing Conditions
4 hours of direct sun
❧

Hardiness
Tender, protect from frosts
❧

When to Buy
Seeds: in winter and spring from catalogues
Plants: from spring to late summer from
nurseries or specialty garden shops
❧

When to Plant
After the last frost
❧

When to Harvest
When leaves are 3 to 5 inches long; harvest
radishes when they reach marble size
❧

EASTER BASKET OF GREENS

Easter arrives with pots of lilies and daffodils for gifts, but why not grow an old-fashioned gardener's basket of greens, complete with dyed Easter eggs, as a gift for friends, relatives, or neighbors. Very simple to grow, the fresh, crisp, young green leaves are the essence of a world newly emerged from winter. Adding a few Johnny-jump-ups provides color, and the blossoms are salad-edible as well. Catalogues sell a variety of radish called 'Easter Egg', which produces charming round radishes in shades from pink to purple. Intersperse some radish seeds among the lettuces. They harvest about three weeks after sowing. ¶ Baskets come with plastic liners, but if you have one without a liner, you can add one yourself. Because the liner prevents excess water from draining from the basket, make sure to water sparingly, checking the potting mix carefully before you water. Add a little note to identify the plants and give directions on how to care for the basket and harvest the lettuces. ¶ **HOW TO DO IT** ¶ In spring, after the last chance of frost, you can safely plant your Easter basket. When the lettuce plants have two sets of true leaves they are ready to plant in the basket. Harden off the lettuces and Johnny-jump-ups for a week by leaving them outside in a protected area during the day and bringing them inside at night. Before planting, submerge the transplants in their containers in a sink or bucket of water until air bubbles cease to appear. ¶ Fill the basket with potting mix to within 2 inches of the rim. Water the mix until it is thoroughly moist. Space the plants evenly in the basket, about 2 to 4 inches apart; place the Johnny-jump-ups at the edge of the basket so they'll drape over the side. Scoop out holes large enough for the roots of the plants. Gently remove each plant and its potting mix from its container, and plant it so that the root ball is level with the surface of the mix. Fill the hole with mix, packing it gently around the ✒

Assorted Lettuces
Lactuca sativa
Johnny-Jump-Ups
Viola tricolor
Radishes
Raphanus sativus

❧

What You Need
12 lettuce plants; 1 packet of radish seeds;
3 Johnny-jump-up plants;
Basket, at least 12 inches in diameter
and 12 inches deep, with a plastic liner;
Potting mix; Liquid organic fertilizer

❧

Recommended Varieties
Lettuce: 'Oak Leaf', 'Deer Tongue';
Radish: 'Easter Egg', 'Iceberg', 'French
Breakfast', 'Sparkler'

❧

Growing Conditions
4 hours of direct sun

❧

Hardiness
Tender, protect from frosts

❧

When to Buy
Seeds: in winter and spring from catalogues
Plants: from spring to late summer from
nurseries or specialty garden shops

❧

When to Plant
After the last frost

❧

When to Harvest
When outer leaves are 3 to 5 inches long;
harvest radishes when they reach
marble size

❧

roots. Pat down the surface and water lightly to fill in any air pockets. Push a radish seed $\frac{1}{4}$ inch down between each plant. ¶ Place the basket where it will receive four hours of sun a day. If the weather is mild, the basket can stay outside in a bright sunny place. Keep the soil moist but not soggy. Fertilize every two weeks with a liquid fertilizer diluted to half strength. ¶ If you are seeding the lettuces directly into the basket, follow the directions for direct seeding on pages 25–7.

Salad bowl mixture of herbs and greens

Many garden pictures, showing long rows of rain-fresh lettuces and richly manured soil, fill the apartment dweller with despair. How, indeed, to grow one's own salad when, if pictures speak the truth, one needs that country acre? Well, it just isn't so. One container can provide fresh salads or a bed of leaves for a dozen sandwiches. ¶ The main trick to supplying your kitchen successfully is keeping a good supply of lettuce growing. Depending upon your appetite for greens, plant two or more garden salad bowls, alternating harvest so the lettuces in one bowl regrow while you gather leaves from the other. Plant lemon thyme and parsley around the edge for a refreshing spike of herbal flavor. ¶ **HOW TO DO IT** ¶ In spring, after the last chance of frost, you can safely plant your garden salad bowl. When the lettuce plants have two sets of true leaves they are ready to plant. Harden them off for a week by leaving them outside in a protected area during the day and bringing them inside at night. Before planting, submerge the lettuce and herb transplants in their containers in a sink or bucket of water until air bubbles cease to appear. ¶ Fill the container with potting mix to within 2 inches of the rim. Water the mix until it is thoroughly moist. Space the plants evenly in the container, about 2 to 4 inches apart. Scoop out holes large enough for the roots of the lettuce and herb plants. Gently remove each plant and its potting mix from its container, and plant it so that the root ball is level with the surface of the mix. Fill the hole with mix, packing it gently around the roots. Pat down the surface and water to fill in any air pockets. ¶ Mulch plants with organic compost spread 1 inch deep. Place the container where it will receive four hours of sun a day and keep the soil moist but not soggy. Fertilize every two weeks with a liquid fertilizer diluted to half strength. ¶ If you are seeding the lettuces directly into the prepared container, follow the directions for direct seeding on pages 25–7.

Assorted Loose-leaf Lettuces
Lactuca sativa
Lemon Thyme
Thymus citriodorus
Italian Flat-leaf Parsley
Petroselinum crispum

What You Need
12 loose-leaf lettuce plants
1 lemon thyme plant
2 Italian flat-leaf parsley plants
Container at least 20 inches in diameter
and 8 inches deep
Potting mix
Organic compost
Liquid organic fertilizer

Recommended Varieties
Lettuce: 'Black-seeded Simpson', 'Four Seasons', 'Biondo Lisce', 'Oak Leaf'

Growing Conditions
4 hours of direct sun

Hardiness
Tender, protect from frosts

When to Buy
From spring to late summer from nurseries
or specialty garden shops

When to Plant
After the last frost

When to Harvest
When outer leaves are 3 to 5 inches long;
snip herbs when plants are 4 inches high

Pea tendrils, flowers, and pods

The Chinese have long regarded the pea plant as a factory of edible parts. The dwarf gray sugar pea best exemplifies why: The young vining tendrils, when just 2 to 3 inches long, have the same crisp texture of the pods and a similar taste. Sweet-tasting pink flowers emerge next; eat some and leave the rest to form crunchy, sugary pods. Set a second pea garden going a few weeks after the first, and you'll have a salad harvest that includes tendrils, flowers, and pods. ¶ Peas grow best during the cool spring or fall seasons. Place the containers where the peas will get morning sun and dappled afternoon shade, and make sure to keep the planting mix moist. Peas need to grow fast, and don't like to dry out. Here's the only warning: Sweet peas, the flowering fragrant peas without edible pods, are poisonous, so make sure children watching or helping you harvest know the difference should you be growing both varieties of pea. ¶ **HOW TO DO IT** ¶ In spring, after the last chance of frost, you can safely plant your peas. When the plants have two sets of true leaves they are ready to set out in containers. Harden them off for a week by leaving them outside in a protected area during the day and bringing them inside at night. Before planting, submerge the transplants in their containers in a sink or bucket of water until air bubbles cease to appear. ¶ Fill each container with potting mix to within 2 inches of the rim. Water the mix until it is thoroughly moist. Space the plants evenly in the container, about 2 to 4 inches apart. Scoop out holes large enough for the roots of the plants. Gently remove each pea plant and its potting mix from its container, and plant it so that the root ball is level with the surface of the mix. Fill the hole with mix, packing it gently around the roots. Pat down the surface and water to fill in any air pockets. ¶ Mulch plants with organic compost spread 1 inch deep. Place the containers where they will receive four hours of sun a day and keep the soil moist but not soggy. Fertilize every two weeks with a liquid fertilizer diluted to half strength.

Dwarf Gray Sugar Peas
Pisum sativum

❧

What You Need
12 plants
2 containers 24 inches in diameter and
18 inches deep
Potting mix
Organic compost
Liquid organic fertilizer

❧

Recommended Variety
'Dwarf Gray Sugar'

❧

Growing Conditions
4 hours of direct sun

❧

Hardiness
Tender, protect from frosts

❧

When to Buy
From spring to late summer from nurseries
or specialty garden shops

❧

When to Plant
After the last frost

❧

When to Harvest
Tendrils at 2 inches, blooms as they
appear, pods at 1 1/2 to 2 inches

❧

WHEELBARROW HARVEST

Using a wheelbarrow for your salad garden is not as kooky as it sounds. It holds enough lettuce for a generous harvest, which is useful if you have a tiny garden but room to park a wheelbarrow. In backyards with only small patches of sun, you can roll your garden to catch that much-needed light as it shifts across the yard. Lastly, in areas of unexpected frosts, being able to wheel the barrow into a protected space overnight can save your harvest. ¶ Most of the older wheelbarrows have holes or cracks so rainwater doesn't collect in them. If yours does not have any holes in the bottom, use a nail and a hammer to make enough holes to provide good drainage. Partially fill the wheelbarrow with water and make sure it will all drain out through your pattern of holes. ¶ **HOW TO DO IT** ¶ In spring, after the last chance of frost, you can safely plant your lettuces. When the plants have two sets of true leaves they are ready to set out in the wheelbarrow. Harden them off for a week by leaving them outside in a protected area during the day and bringing them inside at night. Before planting, submerge the transplants in their containers in a sink or bucket of water until air bubbles cease to appear. ¶ Fill the wheelbarrow with potting mix to within 4 inches of the rim. Water the mix until it is thoroughly moist. Space the plants evenly in the wheelbarrow, about 4 to 6 inches apart. Scoop out holes large enough for the roots of the plants. Gently remove each lettuce plant and its potting mix from its container, and plant it so that the root ball is level with the surface of the mix. Fill the hole with mix, packing it gently around the roots. Pat down the surface and water to fill in any air pockets. ¶ Mulch plants with organic compost spread 2 inches deep. Keep the soil moist but not soggy. Fertilize every two weeks with a liquid fertilizer diluted to half strength. ¶ If you are seeding the lettuce directly into the prepared soil, follow the directions for direct seeding on page 25–7.

Assorted Lettuces

Lactuca sativa

What You Need

24 lettuce plants
1 wheelbarrow, approximately 4 square feet
of planting area
Potting mix
Organic compost
Liquid organic fertilizer

Recommended Varieties

Looseleaf types: 'Oak Leaf', 'Salad Bowl',
'Black-seeded Simpson', 'Brunia', 'Rossimo'
Head types: 'Buttercrunch', 'Sierra',
'Tom Thumb'

Growing Conditions

4 hours of direct sun

Hardiness

Tender, protect from frosts

When to Buy

From spring to late summer from nurseries
or specialty garden shops

When to Plant

After the last frost

When to Harvest

When outer leaves are 3 to 5 inches long

SALAD
GARDENS
IN A PATCH
OF GROUND

The American myth that bigger means better—grand acres better than tidy back gardens, scraps of ground between walk and door, and slender side yards—can be merrily unmasked

by the sheer quantity of greens coaxed from a tiny patch of soil. Even a garden area as small as 2-feet square can grow a profusion of salad greens. ❧ Understanding how greens grow helps you economize on space. Greens don't mind growing closely together because they prefer their soil moist. Thickly sown plants spread their leaves, shading the soil and keeping moisture from evaporating when the sun shines directly on it. Thinning out plants for the salad bowl as they grow larger brings a generous ongoing yield of fresh greens. ❧ Of course, there are just a few gardening tricks to be employed. To keep a small bit of land working all season long, you need to plan for a number of plantings, probably three or four a growing season. Start seeds regularly in propagation trays and set the young plants into the ground as 3- to 4-inch seedlings. Begin early in the season, growing seeds inside, and as soon as the night temperature rises above freezing, set the little plants out. Alternatively, use the cut-and-come-again salad gardening technique: thickly sowing seed over the whole garden, then dividing it into different sections, harvesting the sections one at a time on a rotation, letting each section grow back for further cutting, and replanting after three harvests. ❧ Don't forget about the oft-neglected technique of intercropping. Plant young lettuces between larger plants such as tomatoes, corn, or beans. Within two months, the large plants will fill the space, but until then, you can snugly squeeze in the salad greens, using space that would otherwise be empty. ❧ Lastly, if you love flowers and cannot bear to think of turning over bedding space entirely to greens, consider planting the beautiful ruby-leaved greens among your flowers, or setting out head lettuces to edge a flower bed in soft polka dots. They add color and texture to your flower display as truly as pumpkin-bright marigolds or zinnias, plus you get to serve them up.

Garden of Asian greens

Gardeners raising Asian greens for the first time rave over the beauty of their white-ribbed or red-flushed leaves. Asian greens also have culinary versatility: tender and succulent when young, peppery and hefty as they mature. Leaves not quite tender enough for raw salad make a great wilted salad, stir-fry, or soup. ¶ Many of the Asian greens are mustards; others have less of a peppery zing. Keep an eye out for a mixed selection—the kind that restaurant chefs request—available as seeds or as six-packs. Of course, you can grow the different greens separately and toss them together in the salad bowl. Start picking the outer leaves when they become about 2 inches long. ¶ Asian greens like cool temperatures; in fact they are as hardy as snowboarders, standing up to hard frosts without harm. Sow a late crop at the end of summer to extend your salad garden season into fall. In the spring, the plants grow quickly given lots of water and cool temperatures, but at the first hint of warm days, they bolt, sending out flower stalks. Try cutting off the flower stems as soon as you see them to forestall the plants' decline. Or let them flower and snip off the bright mustard flower heads to dot your salads with color. ¶ **HOW TO DO IT** ¶ In spring, after the last chance of frost, you can safely sow your Asian greens. Make sure to prepare the soil properly (see pages 23–5). ¶ For row planting, draw your finger in a line through the prepared moist soil to create a trough ¼ inch deep. Sow seeds in the trough, spacing them about 1 inch apart. Cover the trough with soil, and pat down firmly. Space the rows 4 inches apart for a tightly planted area, wider if you prefer. ¶ For bed planting, mound the soil in the prepared planting area to form a square bed that is 2 feet by 2 feet and about 6 inches higher than the normal soil level. Sow seeds ✐

Mix of Pak Choi (Bok Choi), Mizuna, Red Mustard, Tat-Soi
Brassica rapa *var.* chinensis, Brassica juncea, Brassica juncea *var.* rugosa, Brassica chiensis

❧

What You Need
1 packet of seeds, Asian mix
4 square feet of prepared ground
Liquid organic fertilizer

❧

Recommended Varieties
Any available

❧

Growing Conditions
4 hours of direct sun

❧

Hardiness
Mature plants are frost hardy

❧

When to Buy
In winter and spring from
catalogues and nurseries

❧

When to Sow
After the last frost

❧

When to Harvest
When outer leaves are 2 inches long

❧

evenly over the bed, about 1 inch apart, and cover them with ¼ inch of soil. Pat the soil down firmly. ¶ Water the planting area thoroughly but gently, so the seeds are not disturbed. Keep the soil moist, but not soggy. Fertilize every two weeks with a liquid fertilizer diluted to half strength. As the plants grow, thin as needed, using the thinnings for salads. For an extended harvest, sow fresh rows or beds every three weeks throughout your planting season.

Cut-and-come-again garden

The cut-and-come-again technique is popular among many of the small market gardeners who raise specialty lettuce to sell to chefs and at farmers markets. It seems too impossible that trimming lettuce beds like a lawn could possibly produce another wave of greens, but it works. Equipped with sharp scissors or a knife, you can begin the trim when the lettuce leaves are about 3 inches high. Cut a section of the bed at a time, for it will take two to three weeks for the lettuces to grow back to their original height. Expect about three harvests from each section. ¶ To continue your harvest all season long, replant one section about one month before you expect the last section to end production. Starting from seeds is preferable to buying transplants because they grow as a thick carpet of plants. If you use transplants, space them about 2 inches apart. The cut-and-come-again technique also works well in container salad gardens. ¶ **HOW TO DO IT** ¶ In spring, after the last chance of frost, you can safely sow your lettuces. Make sure to properly prepare the soil (see pages 23–5). ¶ Mound the soil in the prepared planting area to form a square bed that is 2 feet by 2 feet and about 6 inches higher than the normal soil level. Sow seeds thickly over the bed; cover them with ¼ inch of soil. Pat the soil down firmly. Water thoroughly but gently, so the seeds are not disturbed. Keep the soil moist, but not soggy. Fertilize every two weeks with a liquid fertilizer diluted half strength. When the lettuce leaves are 3 inches long, harvest a section by trimming the leaves back close to the crown, about 1 inch above the soil.

Assorted Loose-leaf Lettuces
Lactuca sativa

What You Need
1 packet of mesclun seeds
4 square feet of prepared ground
Liquid organic fertilizer

Recommended Varieties
Any available

Growing Conditions
4 hours of direct sun

Hardiness
Tender, protect from frosts

When to Buy
In winter and spring from mail-order
catalogues and nurseries

When to Sow
After the last frost

When to Harvest
When outer leaves are 3 to 5 inches long

Mesclun garden

French market gardeners have long upheld a tradition of fine salad gardening. Deliciously flavored salads have held a place almost of royalty in French cuisine, so gardeners have had high standards to live up to. French salads are mostly subtle combinations of flavorful small leaves of lettuces and salad greens—no tomatoes thrown in, no chunks of avocado, but oh those greens. Lots of different varieties add their taste as instruments in an orchestra blend a sound for the whole. Magnifique! ¶ At first imported from Europe, these mixes, called mesclun, have now become the favorites of many of our seed companies. You can plan on your first salad from the harvested baby leaves in thirty-five to forty-five days. Harvest your salad either by picking off the outer leaves from different plants or by using the cut-and-come-again technique (see page 28). ¶ **HOW TO DO IT** ¶ In spring, after the last chance of frost, you can safely sow your lettuces. Make sure to prepare the soil properly (see pages 23–5). ¶ For row planting, draw your finger in a line through the prepared moist soil to create a trough ¼ inch deep. Sow the seeds in the trough, spacing them about 1 inch apart. Cover the trough with soil, and pat down firmly. Space the rows 4 inches apart for a tightly planted area, wider if you prefer. ¶ For bed planting, mound the soil in the prepared planting area to form a square bed that is 2 feet by 2 feet and about 6 inches higher than the normal soil level. Sow seeds evenly over the bed, about 1 inch apart, and cover them with ¼ inch of soil. Pat the soil down firmly. ¶ Water the planting area thoroughly but gently, so the seeds are not disturbed. Keep the soil moist, but not soggy. Fertilize every two weeks with a liquid fertilizer diluted to half strength. As the plants grow, thin as needed, using the thinnings for salads. For an extended harvest, sow fresh rows or beds every three weeks throughout your planting season.

Assorted Lettuces

Lactuca sativa

❧

What You Need

1 packet of mesclun lettuce seeds
4 square feet of prepared ground
Liquid organic fertilizer

❧

Recommended Varieties

Any available

❧

Growing Conditions

4 hours of direct sun

❧

Hardiness

Tender, protect from frosts

❧

When to Buy

In winter and spring from
catalogues and nurseries

❧

When to Sow

After the last frost

❧

When to Harvest

When outer leaves are 3 to 5 inches long

❧

Parterre Garden

In garden parlance, a parterre is an intricately designed bed of flowers or vegetables bordered by tidy low hedges. At the end of the seventeenth century, they were all the rage among the French nobility, with garden designers inventing embroidery or heraldic patterns splendid in plant color and texture. The French chateaus present many superb examples of parterre flower gardens, but none is more delightful than the huge vegetable parterres neatly contained within boxwood hedges at the Chateau de Villandry, near Tours. No one viewing Villandry's Jardin de Potager could say that vegetable gardens need be ordinary and therefore hidden away. ¶ For domestic salad gardens, hedges of parsley make suitably edible and appropriate-sized parterre borders. Set the plants 2 to 3 inches apart to make a hedge quickly. With different colors of lettuces, you can make a jewel mosaic any king or queen would be happy to view. ¶ **HOW TO DO IT** ¶ In spring, after the last chance of frost, you can safely plant your parterre garden. When the lettuce plants have two sets of true leaves they are ready to set out in the garden. Make sure to prepare the soil properly (see pages 23–5). Harden off the lettuce plants for a week by leaving them outside in a protected area during the day and bringing them inside at night. Before planting, submerge the parsley and lettuce transplants in their containers in a sink or bucket of water until air bubbles cease to appear. ¶ Water the planting area until the soil is thoroughly moist. Define the borders of the parterre by planting the parsley around the edge, spacing the plants 2 to 3 inches apart. Then set in the lettuces, alternating the colored lettuces to make a pleasing design. Space the lettuce plants 4 to 6 inches apart. Scoop out ✒

Assorted Lettuces
Lactuca sativa
❧

Curly leaf parsley
Petroselinum crispum
❧

What You Need
12 red-leaved lettuce plants
12 green-leaved lettuce plants
30 parsley plants, curly type
6 square feet of prepared ground
Organic compost
Liquid organic fertilizer
❧

Recommended Varieties
Red-leaf: 'Lollo Rossa', 'Red Sails', 'Samantha'
Green-leaf: 'Salad Bowl', 'Buttercrunch', 'Slobolt'
❧

Growing Conditions
4 hours of direct sun
❧

Hardiness
Parsley: hardy
Lettuces: tender, protect from frosts
❧

When to Buy
From spring to late summer from nurseries or specialty garden shops
❧

When to Plant
After the last frost
❧

When to Harvest
When lettuce leaves are 3 to 5 inches long, and parsley leaves are 4 inches long
❧

holes large enough for the roots of the plants. Gently remove each plant and its potting mix from its container, and plant it so that the root ball is level with the surface of the soil. Fill the hole with soil, packing it gently around the roots. Pat down the surface and water to fill in any air pockets. Mulch plants with organic compost spread 2 inches deep. Keep the soil moist but not soggy, and fertilize every two weeks with a liquid fertilizer diluted to half strength. ¶ If you are seeding the lettuces directly into the prepared garden soil, follow the directions for direct seeding on pages 25–7.

EXOTIC
GREENS

Every cook and gardener must defend against routines that become second nature and therefore, alas, dull. The same old salad, the same old seeds, the same old plantings—such a shame. Gardening must stay an adventure or what was once joy becomes drudgery. Every season, the gardener needs to experiment, never satisfied with just the usual, always trying out something new. Pore over garden catalogues, haunt nurseries, check out farmers markets for specialty produce you might grow in your own garden. Whoever said "Variety is the spice of life" was right, and nowhere is it truer than in salad gardening. ❧ One might think there was nothing much new on the salad scene, but because of the interest among chefs and market gardeners, varieties of new salad greens have arrived recently in droves. Of course, like grandma's clothes left in the attic that come back into style, some of these greens have been lurking in old-fashioned gardens for years. Although they disappeared from seed racks, dedicated gardeners and cooks reseeded their gardens with saved seeds year after year. These heirloom varieties have super flavor and can again be found in nurseries and catalogues. American seed companies have also scoured Europe for the best of the flavorful greens, and with the opening up of Eastern Europe, have brought back even more fixings for our salad bowls. ❧ When you see or taste something new that you like, make sure to note down its name, and try to find seeds or plants. Start a garden journal to record your successes. If you have trouble with a particular crop, write to the seed company. They'll usually provide additional information and advice to aid you.

AMARANTH, A WARM-WEATHER SPINACH

Like many of us, most salad greens wilt and sulk unhappily on the hottest days of summer. A quick hot spell can cause exquisite lettuces to precipitately bolt, growing flower stalks and turning your salad greens from delicately flavored to poisonously bitter-tasting. Even planting them in partial shade may not remedy the problem. Amaranth, however, doesn't at all mind sultry weather; it'll supply you with salad greens throughout the hottest days. ¶ *Amaranth has an ancient history. The Aztecs cultivated and extensively hybridized amaranth for its grain long before Cortez arrived in the 1500s. Supposedly, for festival days they made an amaranth candy shaped like a human body that they ate limb to limb, which so horrified the Spanish missionaries that they promptly banned the candy and the cultivation of the grain.*¶ *A pretty plant, amaranth comes in plain green and red types and also one multicolored form called 'Joseph's Coat', whose jewel-red leaves look somewhat like coleus. Harvest the leaves for salad when the plant is small. Sometimes catalogues list amaranth as 'Chinese Spinach', for the older leaves can be cooked similarly to spinach or added to soup. Amaranth absorbs lots of minerals from the soil, which makes it nutrition-filled, but starves the soil. For the best results, make sure to work in lots of compost before planting and water and fertilize regularly.* ¶ **HOW TO DO IT** ¶ In spring, after the last chance of frost, you can safely sow your amaranth seeds. Make sure to prepare the soil properly (see pages 23–5).¶ For row planting, draw your finger in a line through the prepared moist soil to create a trough ¼ inch deep. Sow the seeds in the trough, spacing them about 1 inch apart. Cover the trough with soil and pat down firmly. Space the rows 4 inches apart for a tightly planted area, wider if you prefer. ¶ For bed planting, mound the soil in the prepared planting area to form a square bed that is 2 feet by 2 feet and about 6 inches higher than the normal soil level. Sow seeds evenly over the bed,

Amaranth, Chinese Spinach
Amaranthus tricolor,
Amaranthus merah

What You Need
1 packet of seeds
4 square feet of prepared ground
Liquid organic fertilizer

Recommended Varieties
'Coleus Leaf Salad', 'Tricolor', 'Traditional', 'Joseph's Coat'

Growing Conditions
4 hours of direct sun

Hardiness
Tender, protect from frosts

When to Buy
In winter and spring from catalogues and nurseries

When to Sow
After the last frost

When to Harvest
When outer leaves are 1 to 2 inches long

about 1 inch apart, and cover them with ¼ inch of soil. Pat the soil down firmly. ¶ Water the planting area thoroughly but gently, so the seeds are not disturbed. Keep the soil moist, but not soggy. Fertilize every two weeks with a liquid fertilizer diluted to half strength. As the plants grow, thin as needed, using the thinnings for salads. For an extended harvest, sow fresh rows or beds every three weeks throughout your planting season.

Arugula, the spicy rocket

This plant has as many names as an aristocrat: It answers to arugula, garden rocket, rocquette, rucola, or Italian cress. Growing wild around the Mediterranean, it soon became a fixture in the cuisines of many Mediterranean countries, hence the different names. The ancient Egyptians and the Romans prepared arugula as an aphrodisiac. The English took to the plant, titling it "rocket," and their cool, wet gardens were a happy home for it, perfectly satisfying its cultivation requirements. The colonists brought arugula to America, making it an imported inhabitant of the New World gardens. ¶ Pungent, peppery arugula grows well in the cool seasons: early spring and autumn. In the height of summer, plant arugula in a partly shady spot, and try to slow the plant's natural inclination to bolt by regularly harvesting the leaves and pinching off the flowers. Arugula is always best harvested for salads when the leaves are no more than 2 to 3 inches tall. After the plant blooms most cooks find the leaves too tough and bitter to use raw. The die-hard arugula lovers sauté the older leaves, blanch and freeze them like spinach, or serve them pureed. ¶ The casual gardener will appreciate arugula's self-seeding weedy habit. Left to bloom, arugula will reliably drop its seeds everywhere, and these will sprout another harvest without any help from the gardener. You can stop it in its tracks by harvesting it before it flowers or by collecting the flowers, before they set seed, for accents in salads, soups, and pastas. ¶ **HOW TO DO IT** ¶ In spring, after the last chance of frost, you can safely sow your arugula seeds. Make sure to prepare the soil properly (see pages 23–5). ¶ For row planting, draw your finger in a line through the prepared moist soil to create a trough ¼ inch deep. Sow the seeds in the trough, spacing them about 1 inch apart. Cover the trough with soil, and pat down firmly. Space the rows 6 inches apart for a tightly planted area, wider if you prefer. ¶ For bed planting, mound the soil in the prepared planting area to form a square bed that is ✒

Arugula, Rocquette, Rucola,
Garden Rocket, Italian Cress
Eruca sativa

What You Need
1 packet of seeds
4 square feet of prepared ground
Liquid organic fertilizer

Recommended Varieties
Any French or Italian varieties

Growing Conditions
4 hours of direct sun

Hardiness
Tender, protect from frosts

When to Buy
In winter and spring from
catalogues and nurseries

When to Sow
After the last frost, then successively
throughout the summer
and early fall

When to Harvest
When outer leaves are 2 inches long

2 feet by 2 feet and about 6 inches higher than the normal soil level. Sow seeds evenly over the bed, about 1 inch apart, and covering them with $\frac{1}{2}$ inch of soil. Pat the soil down firmly. ¶ Water the planting area thoroughly but gently, so the seeds are not disturbed. Keep the soil moist, but not soggy. Fertilize every two weeks with a liquid fertilizer diluted to half strength. As the plants grow, thin as needed, using the thinnings for salads. For an extended harvest, sow fresh rows or beds every three weeks throughout your planting season.

MACHE, THE ALL-SEASON GREEN

Here's another weedy green with a panoply of names: corn salad, lamb's lettuce, rapunzel, feldsalat, even the unappetizing-sounding fetticus. All give testimony to the humble beginnings of this delicious green, which seeds itself freely in cornfields and grazing land. Of course, calling it mache, European style, disguises its weedy origins. Terminology aside, mache serves up deliciously in the kitchen as a leafy base for an upscale BMT (bacon, mache, tomato) or a cold salad of cooked potatoes, carrots, or beets dressed lightly with vinaigrette. Some even cook it like spinach. ¶ A cool-climate character, mache can be sown in a garden bed in earliest spring—although after the last frosts—for an early summer crop, and then again at the beginning of autumn for a winter harvest. Even when the plant has gone to seed, the leaves stay sweet and delicious, so many laissez-faire gardeners let the plants flower and reseed themselves during the busy summertime. Mache survives light frosts readily, and with the addition of a deep mulch and a cold frame, will probably survive all but the coldest winters. Make sure to work lots of organic compost and nitrogen-rich fertilizer into the soil before planting. ¶ **HOW TO DO IT** ¶ In spring, after the last chance of frost, you can safely sow your mache seeds. Make sure to properly prepare the soil (see pages 23–5). ¶ For row planting, draw your finger in a line through the prepared moist soil to create a trough ¼ inch deep. Sow the seeds in the trough, spacing them about 1 inch apart. Cover the trough with soil, and pat down firmly. Space the rows 4 inches apart for a tightly planted area, wider if you prefer. ¶ For bed planting, mound the moist soil in the prepared planting area to form a square bed that is 2 feet by 2 feet and about 6 inches higher than the normal soil ✒

Mache
Valerianella locusta

What You Need
1 packet of seeds
4 square feet of prepared ground
Organic compost
Liquid organic fertilizer

Recommended Varieties
'Coquille', 'd'Etampes', 'Elan', 'Piedmont'

Growing Conditions
4 hours of direct sun

Hardiness
Hardy, depending on variety

When to Buy
In winter and spring from
catalogues and nurseries

When to Sow
After the last frost

When to Harvest
When outer leaves are 3 inches long

level. Sow seeds evenly over the bed, about 1 inch apart, and cover them with ¼ inch of soil. Pat the soil down firmly. ¶ Water the planting area thoroughly but gently, so the seeds are not disturbed. Keep the soil moist, but not soggy. Fertilize every two weeks with a liquid fertilizer diluted to half strength. As the plants grow, thin as needed, using the thinnings for salads. For an extended harvest, sow fresh rows or beds every three weeks throughout your planting season.

OLD-FASHIONED KALE

Gardeners newly introduced to kale are joining the ranks of old-fashioned southern gardeners for whom this tasty green claims a place as a culinary staple. Both plan their spring and winter gardens to make space for this hardy plant that doesn't in the least mind cold weather—in fact, it sweetens after frosts. For the uninitiated or those who have tasted only the pale imitation sold in supermarkets, kale may conjure images of overly hot winter rooms and plates of mushy, long-cooked greens. The news is that homegrown garden kale has been rediscovered as a succulent jaunty-flavored baby salad green, perfect mixed with mild lettuces or served alone as a tasty winter green salad. ¶ Pretty as bright spring flowers and as edible as plain green kale, decorative kale has become widely available as bedding plants in late summer. Set out 4-inch plants and watch them grow to frilly-leaved striped puddles of color as large as 12 inches across. There's even an heirloom variety called 'Walking Stick', which makes a handsome shrub with edible leaves and, as the name implies, grows so tall you can use the stems to fashion a durable cane. If you are short of space for a vegetable garden, use your flower beds or containers for this splashy fall denizen.

¶ **HOW TO DO IT** ¶ In spring, after the last chance of frost, you can safely sow your kale seeds. For a fall crop, start the seeds in mid to late summer. Make sure to prepare the soil properly (see pages 23–5). ¶ For row planting, draw your finger in a line through the prepared moist soil to create a trough ¼ inch deep. Sow the seeds in the trough, spacing them about 1 inch apart. Cover the trough with soil, and pat down firmly. Space the rows 4 inches apart for a tightly planted area, wider if you prefer. ¶ For bed planting, mound the soil in the prepared planting area to form a ✤

Kale
Brassica napus
❧

What You Need
1 packet of seeds
4 square feet of prepared ground
Liquid organic fertilizer
❧

Recommended Varieties
'Red Russian', 'Winterbor',
'Dwarf Blue Curled Scotch'
❧

Growing Conditions
4 hours of direct sun
❧

Hardiness
Hardy, in fact frost sweetens flavor
❧

When to Buy
In winter and spring from
catalogues and nurseries
❧

When to Plant
After the last frost in early spring for
summer crop; in midsummer for fall and
winter crops
❧

When to Harvest
When outer leaves are 3 to 5 inches long
❧

square bed that is 2 feet by 2 feet and about 6 inches higher than the normal soil level. Sow seeds evenly over the bed, about 1 inch apart, and cover them with ¼ inch of soil. Pat the soil down firmly. ¶ Water the planting area thoroughly but gently, so the seeds are not disturbed. Keep the soil moist, but not soggy. Fertilize every two weeks with a liquid fertilizer diluted to half strength. As the plants grow, thin as needed, using the thinnings for salads. ¶ If you are transplanting plants directly into the prepared garden soil, follow the directions on page 27.

Radicchio

The Italians get all the credit for first cultivating this chicory relative which in the United States generally comes in sedate burgundy-red with white veins. The colors of the chicory family duplicate the red, white, and green of the Italian flag, but the green chicory with white veins common in Europe is not widely available here. Some diners daintily pick radicchio out of their salads, their mouths puckering, but with time comes an appreciation for its bittery bite that accentuates a salad. (An equally large number of diners deftly maneuver the radicchio out of the community bowl, to load their own plate.) ¶ Before you turn aside the suggestion of growing this green, unsure whether you want to donate space to a questionable resident, realize that it happily survives winter weather down to 10°F, making it a great winter salad in all but the coldest winter areas. Pop it into vegetable beds otherwise left woefully empty after summer's glory, and have a good crop throughout the winter. Like cabbage, its sturdy leaves are delicious baked, grilled, stuffed, or sautéed. ¶ **HOW TO DO IT** ¶ In spring, after the last chance of frost, you can safely sow your raddichio seeds. ¶ Make sure to prepare the soil properly (see pages 23–5). ¶ For row planting, draw your finger in a line through the prepared moist soil to create a trough ¼ inch deep. Sow the seeds in the trough, spacing them about 1 inch apart. Cover the trough with soil, pat down firmly. Space the rows 4 inches apart for a tightly planted area, wider if you prefer. ¶ For bed planting, mound the moist soil in the prepared planting area to form a square bed that is 2 feet by 2 feet and about 6 inches higher than the normal soil level. Sow seeds evenly over the bed, about 1 inch apart, and cover them with ¼ inch of soil. Pat the soil down firmly. ¶ Water the planting ✎

Radicchio
Cichorium intybus
❧

What You Need
1 packet of seeds
4 square feet of prepared ground
Liquid organic fertilizer
❧

Recommended Varieties
'Guilio', 'Rossano', 'Nerome Di Trevoso'
❧

Growing Conditions
4 hours of direct sun
❧

Hardiness
Hardy down to 10°F, depending on variety
❧

When to Buy
In winter and spring from mail-order catalogues and nurseries
❧

When to Sow
After the last frost
❧

When to Harvest
When outer leaves are 3 inches long
❧

area thoroughly but gently, so the seeds are not disturbed. Keep the soil moist, but not soggy. Fertilize every two weeks with a liquid fertilizer diluted half strength. As the plants grow, thin as needed, using the thinnings for salads. For an extended harvest, sow fresh rows or beds every three weeks throughout your planting season. ¶ Radicchio can also be grown from transplants set out during July for a fall harvest. If you are transplanting plants directly into the prepared garden soil, follow the directions on page 27.

Sorrel

Sorrel is prized by the French, who cook it for fragrant lemony soups, a puree accompaniment to veal dishes, and a tart side dish perfect with fish. Alexandre Dumas, the nineteenth-century fiction writer who in his spare time penned a culinary dictionary, described a standard French sorrel recipe: chopped sorrel, chard, chervil, and lettuce sautéed with butter, then thickened with cream and egg yolk. However grand the culinary hoopla over cooked sorrel, the young tender leaves are equally renowned as small taste bites in salads. Their citrus burst, like peacocks among chickens, contributes a shockingly bright taste to the blander lettuces. ¶ The cook must include sorrel in the garden because it is rarely available in American specialty markets, and with good reason. Sorrel wilts quickly after harvest, so it is to your benefit to have a patch growing just steps from the kitchen. ¶ Although the taste is aristocratic, in truth sorrel is no fussier than many weeds. Given fertile soil and kept moist, it may even become tiresomely invasive. Digging out superfluous plants in spring and cutting off seed stalks in the summer will keep it under control. In mild-winter areas, it stays evergreen; in frosty areas, it dies down but returns in spring. Gardeners living in very cold winter areas should let the plants die down in fall, then dig up the roots and overwinter them indoors, in a cool place with temperatures above 45°F. Although sorrel is a perennial, coming back year after year, after three years let the plant flower and drop its seed. Reestablish your sorrel bed with the new seedlings. ¶ **HOW TO DO IT** ¶ In spring, after the last chance of frost, you can safely plant your sorrel. Harden the plants off for a week by leaving them outside in a protected area during the day and bringing them inside at night. Before planting, submerge the transplants in their containers in a sink or bucket of water until air bubbles cease to ✐

Sorrel
Rumex acetosa
❧

What You Need
4 sorrel plants
4 square feet of prepared ground
Organic compost
Liquid organic fertilizer
❧

Recommended Varieties
French sorrel
❧

Growing Conditions
4 hours of direct sun
❧

Hardiness
Tender, protect from frosts
❧

When to Buy
In spring from nurseries or specialty garden shops
❧

When to Plant
After the last frost
❧

When to Harvest
When outer leaves are 3 to 5 inches long
❧

appear. ¶ Mound the moist soil in the prepared planting area to form a square bed that is 2 feet by 2 feet and about 6 inches higher than the normal soil level. Scoop out holes large enough for the roots of the plants. Space the plants evenly, about 4 to 6 inches apart. Gently remove each sorrel plant and its potting mix from its container, and plant it so that the root ball is level with the surface of the soil. Fill the hole with soil, packing it gently around the roots. Pat down the surface, and water to fill in any air pockets. ¶ Mulch plants with organic compost spread 2 inches deep. Keep the soil moist, but not soggy. During the spring while the plant is growing, fertilize every three weeks with a liquid fertilizer diluted to half strength.

FRESH
SALADS
FROM THE
GARDEN

**W**hen young Victorian ladies grew up, they were admonished never to be seen outside the family doors "undressed," that was, without hat, hankie, gloves, and purse. So, too, it's de rigueur that salads appear slightly slicked with a fragrant emulsion of vinegar, oil, and subtle seasonings when they make their appearance at the table. Continuing the metaphor, be mindful of one old piece of etiquette: It's better to be underdressed than overdressed. As inappropriate as a tea gown at a pool party, an overdressed salad is a sad state of affairs; don't ruin things by letting guests find gobs of vinaigrette puddling in the bottom of the salad bowl. ❧ Bypass dressings that obscure the delicate flavors of homegrown salad greens. Thick, mayonnaise-based, overly garlicky sauces or heavy blue-cheese dressings obscure the subtle flavors of freshly picked homegrown produce. For those who love intensely flavored dressings, apply them to bland store-bought lettuces such as iceberg and romaine, which give a crunchy, vibrant texture in perfect harmony with the strong-flavored dressings. ❧ Controversy swirls over the proper placement of salads within the rhythm of the meal. American tradition has the salad as precursor to the main entree, its role to heighten the palate for the more heavily flavored main course. Coming first, the delicate fresh salad flavor cannot be obscured by the more highly seasoned main dish, much like drinking a light white wine before proceeding to a richer red one. European tradition, dating from the Roman conquest and influenced by seventeenth-century medical convictions, has salad trudging along after the main course, cleansing and lightening the lingering memory of the entree on the digestion. ❧ Remember, flavors and tastes have changed through the ages, and so have the ingredients and balance of dishes within the meal. There are a number of totally content diners who prefer to dish up their salad alongside their spaghetti for pleasant Sunday night suppers. So who is correct? Your personal style and

preference and, to some degree, the occasion, should hold sway. Formal dinners staged in courses certainly call for a different treatment than an informal garden luncheon. Try the placement as you wish; practice will bring good judgment. ❧ Delicate salad leaves crisp and fresh from the garden are best broken with your hands rather than cut with a knife, which may bruise them. Most salad eaters find it hard to juggle leaves larger than fork-size bits, so break large leaves into pieces. Of course, crisphead lettuce such as iceberg can be cut with a knife into confetti slivers, perfect for nests underneath cold meat or chicken salads or for lining sandwiches. ❧ Because you need only a smidgen of oil and vinegar to lightly coat salad greens, buy the very best, for their flavors must be as refined and delicate as your tender, freshly picked greens. Inferior, too-sharp vinegar or slightly rancid oils shout out their off-flavors immediately, ruining your salad. Oils oxidize and become rancid when kept open, in bright light, or over too long a time. Buy small amounts of fine-quality salad oils, whether virgin olive oil or nut oils, and store them tightly stoppered in glass containers in a cool, dark spot. Any off-taste and you must jettison them immediately. ❧ If you grew up in the fifties, you might remember waiters performing an elaborate ballet with silver tongs and a salad bowl, chilled perfunctorily on crushed ice, and separate dishes of salad greens, croutons, and carrot slivers. Sometimes this performance was reserved just for Caesar salads, sometimes even the ordinary house salad was tossed as fine entertainment. Your salads at home can be combined without such fuss but with superb results. In truth, behind kitchen doors in the fanciest restaurants, salad chefs are probably using their hands to toss the leaves, so as not to bruise them. You can use any large spoon and fork you have handy; just toss gently. Your bowl can be wood, metal, or ceramic. Rinse out wooden bowls thoroughly after use with simple hot water (detergent can enter the wood, continuing to lend its soapy taste). Wipe the wood dry with a paper towel to remove all traces of oil, which if left, can give off a rancid taste over time. ❧ Until you feel confident, mix your dressing separately, then pour half of it into the bottom of the salad bowl. Add the greens, well washed and dried, to the bowl and toss gently but thoroughly. Taste a leaf, and decide whether you need more dressing. The leaf should be only lightly coated, just so you subtly taste the dressing married to the flavor of the green. If you so desire, add more dressing and again toss the greens thoroughly. Salt and pepper to taste at the very last. Serve immediately. Salads that sit become unsavory and unappealing; the greens wilt. ❧ Reassure diners concerned about the fat content of your salad dressing that a single portion of salad contains a minimal amount of oil, because you have carefully avoided pouring on too much dressing. Let's none of us go as far as the television chef who tosses a salad and then spins the tossed greens almost dry in a salad spinner. Adding just enough dressing to lightly coat your salad will leave you with a delightfully low-fat dish, flavorful, and very nourishing. ❧ A last note about the bottom of the salad bowl and garlic. A time-honored tradition has the salad maker rubbing a peeled, cut piece of garlic over the bottom of the salad bowl. The dressing is then mixed in the bottom of the bowl, and the greens added and tossed. The great success of this method is that it imbues the salad with just a whiff of garlic. Raw garlic squeezed through a press, chopped, or smashed, and added to a salad dressing has an unpleasant harsh taste many diners find overly strong and, later on, too vivid an indigestible memory. Experiment with adding garlic to your salads if you like the taste, or try oil infused with garlic for a more subtle flavor.

OILS

Nuts, seeds, and certain fruits when mechanically pressed give up oil. How that oil is processed and refined greatly influences the final flavor. Supermarket shelves are now crowded with a variety of oils made from sunflower, safflower, avocado, grape seed, and olive. Olive oil is one of the oldest processed oils known to humankind. The bottom of the Mediterranean is littered with shards of olive oil containers sunk in the terrible shipwrecks of the Minoans. Egyptian papyrus records list stores of olive oil belonging to the original oil barons. Even today, the rich taste of good olive oil underscores the taste of salad in a satisfactory manner and is the oil of choice for most fine salads.

¶ True extra virgin olive oil is the product of the first olive pressing; it's a deep-colored, rich-tasting oil. Regulations now allow for it to be blended with refined grade olive oil, from later pressings, and the blend also labeled "extra virgin." Very high-quality extra virgin olive oil, made exclusively from a first pressing, is expensive. In Italy it's served as a condiment, a few drops sprinkled over hot pasta or composed salads. Try different brands to find a taste that pleases. Refined grade olive oil barely reflects its olive heritage, but for some salads, a plainer tasting oil allows the full flavor of the greens to come through. Experiment with other types of oils so your salad making never becomes mechanical.

¶ Flavored oils add a nuance, a subtle layering of taste that can make salad eaters perk up with surprise. "My this salad tastes delicious, just what did you do differently?" is a common question. Elegantly packaged and expensive to buy in the stores, these commercially produced oils are often made from indifferent ingredients.

VINEGARS

Sugars in fruits and grains ferment to create alcohol, and if the alcohol is exposed to bacteria, it converts to acetic acid or vinegar—from the French *vin aigre*, meaning sour wine. Anyone who has tried to age wine knows that bacteria drifting in the air can quickly metabolize the alcohol to vinegar.

¶ Many types of vinegar derive from fermented fruits, for example, cider vinegar from apples, and red or white wine vinegar from grapes. Malt vinegars come from fermented grain alcohol, such as beer and whiskey. Rice wine vinegar comes from sake. Look for the distinctive taste in each type of vinegar.

¶ Don't confuse the different vinegar types with flavored vinegars. Fruits, herbs, even fragrant rose petals steeped in vinegars will add their own distinctive essence. Tarragon vinegar is the flavored vinegar renowned in French vinaigrettes. Raspberry vinegar had a trendy run in metropolitan restaurants on everything from radicchio leaves to venison steaks. Chili vinegars are a refreshing replacement for the ubiquitous spicy red-pepper commercial sauces. Try creating flavored vinegars yourself by marinating the fruits or herbs in vinegar until the flavor develops that satisfies you.

¶ Taste the vinegar you plan to use before you add it to your vinaigrette. Some brands are very acidic, and using them in the exact amounts the recipe requests will make a caustic dressing. Other brands seem mild and will not add the zip to balance the flavor of the oil. Salad making is an inexact science, so for best results, be ready to adjust any recipe to the specific flavors of your vinegars and oils. Here is a starter list of some widely available vinegars to try in your salad dressings.

¶ *Apple cider vinegar:* Made from fermented cider, the commercial product has a tested acidity of five percent. The cider flavor mildly underscores the taste of pickles or herb vinegars for a rich-tasting result. Try different brands to find one with a refined, light taste.

¶ *Balsamic vinegar:* Real *aceto balsamico* comes from an ancient tradition of aging wine vinegar into a very dark, almost viscous liquid so rich and precious only a few drops are used as a condiment. The vinegar reduces through natural evaporation in a series of casks, each cask being made from a different type of wood and getting progressively smaller as the vinegar becomes more and more concentrated. This nectar comes in a very small bottle with a big price tag. More widely available are blends of the aged with young vinegars generously used in salad dressings. The dark color of balsamic vinegar looks unattractive on light-colored salads.

¶ *Champagne vinegar:* A delicious light-tasting vinegar. Use it in very subtle dressings with an equally subtle oil.

¶ *Red wine vinegar:* Usually milder in taste than white wine vinegar, this vinegar makes a smooth vinaigrette that doesn't catch in the throat.

¶ *Sherry vinegar:* A rich-tasting vinegar with nutty aftertones.

¶ *White vinegar, often called distilled vinegar:* Five percent acid, this vinegar has a strong, flat taste, but because it's clear, it does not affect the color of pickled fruits and vegetables.

¶ *White wine vinegar:* Like different grades of wine, white wine vinegar runs from sophisticated subtle blends to screechingly horrible, mouth-puckering acid hits. Sample different brands, and always taste-check the proportion of vinegar to oil in each recipe.

¶ Of course, citrus juices have long been used to supply the acid balance in a vinaigrette. Freshly squeezed lemon juice, augmented with tendrils of zest, makes a refreshing change to vinegar in salad dressings. Many wine lovers prefer lemon juice to distilled vinegars, for they feel vinegars ruin the palate, wiping out the fine distinctions between wines. Citrus vinaigrettes are particularly successful with meat or poultry salads. Look for unusual citrus such as kumquats, rangpur limes, blood oranges, or key limes to add zesty flavors to your salad dressings.

VINAIGRETTES

Michele Anne Jordan, a noted food writer, reminded me that a vinaigrette originally was a small silver box with a chased lid. My mother once showed me one handed down from a forgotten ancestor and, sadly, now lost. Only about an inch long, thin and decorous as a modest pillbox, its bright silver top was cut out like a stencil. These boxes were essential armaments for ladies walking short distances from their carriages to their destination, when the gutters ran with raw sewage and the horses added smelly muck to the streets. Ladies gratefully held the little boxes up to their noses, for the bits of linen or cotton sprinkled with vinegar that lay inside masked the foul odors of the air.

¶ Now the name applies to a graceful mix of oil and vinegar, usually in the proportion of three parts oil to one part vinegar and blended with taste hits of garlic, onion, mustard, herbs, salt and pepper, sugar, honey, or even molasses. The French-style vinaigrette diverges from the English and American traditions of boiled cream— or mayonnaise-based dressings. In these days of rationing fat and salt, careful cooks have a tendency to cheat on the proportions, cutting down the oil and leaving out the salt. Tradition has had lots of practice though, and your salad will suffer from such thrift. Remember that a well-dressed salad needs only a minimal amount of dressing to coat the leaves, so take heart and enjoy eating your greens with a well-balanced vinaigrette.

Lemon Fragrant Oil

A vinaigrette made with lemon oil provides the aromatic hint of lemon without unbalancing the dressing with too much acid from vinegars. Just a whiff of acid balances the oil. ¶ Make flavored oils swiftly in your own kitchen, while you wait for the coffee water to boil, simply by adding blanched citrus peel to oil and letting it steep overnight. Decant the oil into another bottle, discarding the peel. Make only a small amount at a time, label the date you made it, store in the refrigerator for no more than a week. ¶ **HOW TO DO IT** ¶ Make sure your jar is clean and dry. Peel the lemon thinly; then make sure to remove any pith, the white part under the peel. Add the lemon peel to boiling water and blanch for 2 minutes. Drain the peel, pat it dry with paper towel, and add to the oil. Let oil stand overnight to steep. In the morning, discard the peel, tightly stopper the bottle, and store it in the refrigerator. Use the oil within one week. ¶ Note: Steeping low-acid fresh ingredients in olive oil, an anaerobic (oxygen-free) environment can result in the growth of harmful bacteria. Make sure to follow only the prescribed method.

What You Need
Quart jar with lid
Peel of 2 lemons, the pith removed
3 cups olive oil
750-ml bottle

Full-flavored Tarragon Vinegar

Stocking your pantry with herb-infused vinegars is incredibly simple. If you use a vinegar with a five percent acidity, there is no need to remove the tarragon unless you wish to—the acidity protects the vinegar from mold. Use small decorative bottles to store your vinegar in, but make enough to last the long winter months, until your herb garden is producing its bounty again. Flavored vinegars make wonderful gifts. ¶ **HOW TO DO IT** ¶ Toast the mustard seeds in a small sauté pan just until they begin to pop. They'll continue to cook after you take them off the heat, and if they become too dark, they'll taste bitter. Set the seeds aside to cool. ¶ Place all the seasonings in a quart jar. Peel the lemon thinly, then make sure to remove any pith, the white part beneath the peel. Pour over the vinegar. Make sure to push down the tarragon so the vinegar covers it totally. Seal with a lid. Place the jar on a windowsill for two weeks. Test the vinegar after one week by tasting a small amount with a piece of French bread. Continue to let the vinegar steep, sampling it regularly until it is flavored to your satisfaction. Decant the vinegar into a 750-ml bottle. Tightly stopper the bottle, label and date it, and store it in a cool, dark place. ¶ Note: Use this recipe as a guide to making other flavored vinegars. Try fruit flavors such as raspberry or blackberry, herbs such as lemon thyme or purple basil (a gorgeous deep purply red color), and blends of herbs and fruits such as rosemary and lemon, or fig and rosemary. Tarragon, basil, rosemary, chive-blossom, rose-petal, and nasturtium-blossom vinegars can be quickly made and stored. The herbal essence is most intense for the first months, then fades to a subtle flavoring.

What You Need

1 tablespoon mustard seeds
Quart jar with lid
6 sprigs tarragon, each about 4 inches long
1 clove garlic, peeled and cut into 4 pieces
1 teaspoon whole peppercorns
1 small dried chili pepper
2 inches lemon peel, the pith removed
3½ cups cider vinegar
750-ml wine bottle

Asian Greens with Sesame Vinaigrette

Asian greens, with their mustard heritage, have a zippy taste that stands up to an assertive sesame salad dressing. The Asian sesame oil for this vinaigrette is pressed from toasted sesame seeds and is a tastebud–world away from the oil made from untoasted seeds. Buy dark amber-colored oil in the smallest bottle available. You'll need only a small amount of the strongly fragrant oil at a time, although once you've tasted it, you may decide to use it in marinades, as a glazing for roasted poultry and fish, or in myriad other ways. ¶ **HOW TO DO IT** ¶ Toast the sesame seeds in a small sauté pan just until they turn a light golden color, about 3 minutes. They'll continue to cook after you take them off the heat, and if they become too dark, they'll taste bitter. Set the seeds aside to cool. ¶ Mix together the oils, lemon juice, soy sauce, and minced garlic. Squeeze the grated ginger in your fist to extract the ginger juice and add the juice to the dressing. Add the cilantro, if desired, and thoroughly whisk all the ingredients together. Season with salt and pepper. ¶ Place the toasted sesame seeds, salad greens, and sliced scallions in a bowl. Rewhisk the dressing, pour it over the greens, and toss well. Serves four as a salad course.

What You Need

2 tablespoons sesame seeds

4 cups washed and dried mixed Asian greens, such as mizuna, tat-soi, red mustard, pak choi, and kale

2 green scallions, trimmed and thinly sliced

❧

Vinaigrette

3 tablespoons olive oil

1 tablespoon Asian sesame oil

2 tablespoons freshly squeezed lemon juice

1 tablespoon soy sauce

1 garlic clove, finely minced

1-inch knob of ginger, grated

2 teaspoons finely chopped cilantro, optional

Salt and freshly ground pepper to taste

❧

CLASSIC GARDEN SALAD WITH EDIBLE FLOWERS

On sultry summer days, appetites flag, and somehow the age-old folk talk of the cooling power of lettuces seems perfectly wise. On days like these, a simple salad may answer for all of luncheon or a refreshing course in a patio dinner. Alternatively, salad travels easily for a picnic beside a cool-sounding brook, a nice variant to the picnic sandwich. Store the ingredients in a plastic bag, and carry the bag in a cooler. Toss with the premixed vinaigrette just before serving. ¶ Use this classic recipe as a base for your creative impulses. Add crumbled feta or goat cheese, chopped bits of chicken breast or, for an updated Niçoise, hard-boiled eggs, cooked new potatoes, olives, and cooled, grilled fish. ¶ **HOW TO DO IT** ¶ Place the greens and flowers in a salad bowl. ¶ Add the vinegar, salt, and pepper to a small mixing bowl. Whisk them together thoroughly. Slowly add the oil, continuing to whisk until the oil is incorporated into the vinegar. Taste again for seasonings. ¶ Thoroughly toss the vinaigrette with the mixed greens and serve immediately. Serves four as a salad course, two as a main course.

What You Need

4 cups mixed greens and edible flowers such as viola, calendula, borage, or rose petals, washed, dried, and torn into bite-sized pieces

❧

Vinaigrette

2 tablespoons tarragon white wine vinegar
Salt and freshly ground pepper to taste
6 tablespoons extra virgin olive oil

❧

Grilled Garden Green Salad

Grilling fresh greens takes a dab hand. You need to regulate the amount of oil on the greens and control the fire so as to add a touch of smokiness to them without burning them. Still, with a little concentration, you can make a novel and delicious warm green salad. Use the strong-textured greens—radicchio, mustard, romaine, and kale—that can stand up to grilling. Soft, buttery leaves melt on the grill. Grill the radicchio and romaine sliced in half lengthwise. Remember to leave the greens on the grill for just a short time, giving them the brown crisped look of grilled vegetables. ¶ **HOW TO DO IT** ¶ Start a charcoal or gas grill. ¶ Lightly brush the greens with olive oil. When you can hold your hand over the top of the grill and spell M-i-s-s-i-s-s-i-p-p-i, place the leaves on top of the grill and let them cook for 1 to 3 minutes on each side, or until slightly browned but not blackened. If you are using the radicchio or romaine sliced in half, grill it for 3 to 5 minutes on each side. ¶ Remove the greens from the grill. Coarsely chop them into large, 2 inch-by-2 inch, pieces. Toss them with 1 tablespoon of oil, and salt and pepper. Add balsamic vinegar to taste, about 1 teaspoon. Serves four as a salad or side dish.

What You Need

16 stalks of greens, washed and dried; or
4 radicchio or romaine lettuces sliced in
half lengthwise
1 tablespoon olive oil
❧

Vinaigrette

1 tablespoon olive oil
Salt and pepper to taste
1 teaspoon balsamic vinegar, or to taste
❧

WINTER PARSLEY SALAD WITH HERB-CRUSTED GOAT CHEESE

Sometimes in winter, salad making is discouraging. Store lettuces, being properly out of season, look drab and unappealing. Yet parsley will grow fresh and hearty all year long in your garden, even if only in containers and greenhouses in snowy locales. ¶ Filled with vitamin C and minerals, parsley salad is perfect for the winter blahs and shopping blues. The Greeks hailed the medicinal qualities of parsley and, instead of laurel wreaths, wove parsley crowns to adorn winning athletes. Although it's now less exalted, often no more than a small, decorative green gewgaw on a serving platter, the flavor is delicious. ¶ This salad balances the piquant flavor of parsley against the equally assertive goat cheese and herbs. Without the goat cheese, the flavors still sing, so even if the larder is empty of cheese, serve up the salad without a murmur of apology. ¶ **HOW TO DO IT** ¶ Preheat the oven to 350°F. ¶ Toss the bread crumbs with the oil and herbs. Gently press this crumb mixture around the goat cheese to make a thin crust. Bake the goat cheese on a cookie sheet for 15 to 20 minutes, or until the crust becomes golden brown. ¶ Add the vinegar, mustard, sugar, salt, and pepper to a small mixing bowl. Whisk them together thoroughly. Slowly, add the oil, continuing to whisk until the oil is incorporated into the vinegar mixture. Taste for seasonings. ¶ Toss the vinaigrette with the coarsely chopped parsley. Divide the parsley salad onto four plates. Cut the warm goat cheese into quarters. On each plate, snuggle a cheese portion next to the parsley salad. Sprinkle the cheese with the finely chopped parsley. Serves four as a salad course.

What You Need

¼ cup fresh bread crumbs, finely grated
2 tablespoons olive oil
1 tablespoon finely chopped fresh thyme, or ½ teaspoon dried
1 tablespoon finely chopped fresh rosemary, or ½ teaspoon dried
1 round, about 8 ounces, goat cheese, chilled
4 cups curly parsley, stemmed and coarsely chopped
1 tablespoon finely chopped parsley

Vinaigrette

4 tablespoons balsamic vinegar
½ teaspoon Dijon mustard
¼ teaspoon sugar
Salt and freshly ground pepper to taste
¼ cup extra virgin olive oil

Ruby-leaf Lettuce with Blood Oranges, Fennel, and Parmesan

Who says salads must come only in monochrome green? In this salad, vibrant red lettuce leaves echo red-hued oranges. The white-green slender crescents of fennel and the rich buttermilk-colored slivers of parmesan add a lightness to the burgundy colors. The flavors also marry well together. Blood oranges are available only in the early part of the year, so substitute ruby grapefruit as necessary. ¶ **HOW TO DO IT** ¶ Using a sharp paring knife, carefully cut off the orange peel, just as you would peel an apple, in concentric circles working from the top to the bottom. Trim off any white pith that remains on the fruit and discard it with the peel. Holding one prepared orange in your hand over a bowl, cut in between the white membrane surrounding each segment, free the bright, juicy, fresh, half moon–shaped orange section and let it slip into the bowl. Continue until you have sliced and emptied all the segments and only the white membrane remains, looking somewhat like the pages of a book. Squeeze any juice remaining into the bowl and discard the membrane. Repeat with the other orange. ¶ Drain off the juice and place the orange pieces in the bottom of the salad bowl. Add the vinegar, salt, and pepper to a small mixing bowl. Whisk them together thoroughly. Slowly, add the oil, continuing to whisk until the oil is incorporated into the vinegar. Taste for seasonings, adding the drained orange juice to taste. ¶ Add the lettuce, fennel, and red onion to the salad bowl. Toss with the vinaigrette. Serve onto plates. Place two or three shavings of parmesan cheese on top of each salad. Serves four as a salad course, two as a main course.

What You Need

2 blood oranges
4 cups red-leaf lettuce, washed, dried, and torn into bite-sized pieces
1 fennel bulb, sliced into thin slivers (about 2 cups)
⅓ cup thinly sliced red onion rings
2 ounces parmesan or reggiano, thinly shaved (8 to 12 thin shavings)

Vinaigrette

2 tablespoons red wine vinegar
Salt and freshly ground pepper to taste
6 tablespoons extra virgin olive oil
Juice drained from the oranges, to taste

Old-fashioned Wilted Greens with Bacon and Garlic Chips

The popularity of wilted salads faded in the mid-seventies; the use of bacon grease in the dressing seemed jaded and unhealthy. However, their reputation has now been restored by wilting the greens lightly in olive oil and adding the crisped bits of bacon, cooked separately and drained thoroughly, at the last moment. Using this method, the salad still has a rich meaty flavor without the bacon grease. Although medical studies are conflicting, garlic is deemed to lower cholesterol, so if the bits of bacon worry you, add more garlic to offset their effect. In fall, winter, or early spring, this salad seems both refreshing and hearty. ¶ **HOW TO DO IT** ¶ Heat a sauté pan over medium heat and cook the bacon until it is brown and crisp, about 5 minutes per side. Remove the bacon from the pan with a slotted spoon and drain on paper towels. When the bacon has cooled, break it into small pieces. ¶ Add the garlic slices to the sauté pan and cook over medium heat, stirring frequently, until they are just golden brown, about 5 minutes. They will continue to cook after you take them off the heat, and if they become too dark, they'll taste bitter. Take the pan off the heat and remove the garlic from the pan with a slotted spoon. Discard the oil, wiping the pan clean with paper towels. ¶ Add the vinegar, sugar, salt, and pepper to a small mixing bowl. Whisk them together thoroughly. Slowly add the oil, continuing to whisk until the oil is incorporated into the vinegar. Taste for seasonings. ¶ Warm the vinaigrette over medium heat and add the bacon bits and the garlic chips, stirring constantly. When the bacon and garlic are warmed through, take the pan off the heat. Place the greens in a salad bowl. Toss with the warmed vinaigrette, adjust the seasonings, and serve immediately. Serves four as salad course, two as a main course.

What You Need
4 slices bacon or pancetta, about 4 ounces
6 cloves of garlic, peeled and sliced 1/4 inch thick
4 cups washed and dried mixed greens: young leaves of kale, chard, arugula, and mizuna
❧

Vinaigrette
2 tablespoons balsamic vinegar
1/4 teaspoon sugar
Salt and freshly ground pepper to taste
6 tablespoons olive oil
❧

Seed and Plant Sources

Most companies test-grow their seeds before they sell them. Although they offer seeds to grow in gardens all over America, they know by experience what grows well in their area. Call the companies closest to you if you need suggestions about salad greens successful in your climate. Some companies charge for their catalogue. Call first to check prices and availability.

Bountiful Gardens
18001 Shafer Ranch Road
Willits, CA 95490
707 459-6410
Seeds, garden craft items, tools, and supplies.

W. Atlee Burpee & Co.
PO Box 5114
Warminster, PA 18974
215 674-9633
A standard selection of seeds.

The Cook's Garden
PO Box 535
Londonderry, VT 05148-0535
802 824-3400
A superb seed selection of greens plus different types of mesclun mixes and Asian mixes. A must-have catalogue for the salad gardener.

DeGiorgi Seed Company
6011 N Street
Omaha, NE 68117-1634
800 858-2580
Seeds of alliums, chicories, kale, lettuces, and herbs.

Foxhill Farm
443 West Michigan Avenue
PO Box 9
Parma, MI 49269
517 531-3179
Fax 517 531-3179
Plants throughout the year. Many varieties of basil and rosemary.

Heirloom Garden Seeds
PO Box 138
Guerneville, CA 95446
707 869-0967
Heirloom and old-fashioned nonhybrid seeds, ten varieties of basil.

Johnny's Selected Seeds
310 Foss Hill Road
Albion, ME 04910
207 437-9294
Seeds and sets for shallots, five types of basil, and many excellent varieties of greens, including amaranth.

Kitazawa Seed Company
1111 Chapman Street
San Jose, CA 95126
*An excellent assortment of Asian greens, plus
several varieties of radishes.*

Nichols Garden Nursery
1190 North Pacific Highway
Albany, OR 97321
503 928-9280
*A good seed selection of Asian greens, radicchio,
and lettuces, and seeds plus plants of herbs
(herb plants shipped only in spring and fall).*

Seeds of Change
1364 Rufina Circle #5
Santa Fe, NM 87501
505 438-8080
*Organic seeds with a selection of amaranth,
lettuces, and Asian greens.*

Shepherd's Garden Seeds
6116 Highway 9
Felton, CA 95018
408 335-5216
Fax 408 335-2080
*Quality seeds featuring international varieties of
unusually fine taste, including a number of the
mesclun blends. Every salad gardener should try
these seeds.*

Territorial Seed Co.
PO Box 157
Cottage Grove, OR 97424
503 942-9547
*An extensive list of greens for cool-summer
climates, plus four hundred varieties of
other specialty seeds.*

BIBLIOGRAPHY

Brennan, Georgeanne.
*Potager: Fresh Garden Cooking
in the French Style.*
San Francisco: Chronicle Books, 1992.

Brennan, Georgeanne, and
Mimi Luebbermann.
Little Herb Gardens.
San Francisco: Chronicle Books, 1993.

Coleman, Eliot.
The New Organic Grower's Four Season Harvest.
Post Mills, Vermont: Chelsey Green
Publishing Company, 1992.

Colman, Louis.
Alexandre Dumas' Dictionary of Cuisine.
New York: Simon & Schuster, 1958.

Creasy, Rosalind.
Cooking from the Garden.
San Francisco: Sierra Club Books,
1988.

Gershuny, Grace, and
Deborah L. Martin.
The Rodale Book of Composting.
Emmaus, Pennsylvania: Rodale
Publishing, 1992.

Hooker, Margaret Huntington.
*Early American Cookery or
Ye Gentlewoman's Housewifery.*
Scotia, New York: Americana Review,
1981.

Hortus Third Dictionary.
New York: Macmillan, 1976.

Jordan, Michele Anna.
The Good Cook's Book of Oil & Vinegar.
Reading, Massachusetts:
Addison-Wesley, 1992.

Kraus, Sibella.
Greens, A Country Garden Cookbook.
San Francisco: CollinsPublishing, 1993.

Larkcom, Joy.
The Salad Garden.
New York: The Viking Press, 1984.

Lima, Patrick.
The Natural Food Garden.
Rocklin, California: Prima Publishing,
1992.

McGee, Harold.
*On Food and Cooking, the Science
and Lore of the Kitchen.*
New York: Collier Books, 1984.

Index

Acknowledgments

Like a garden patch grown with a mesclun salad mix, the contributors to this book have added the textures and colors of their different wisdom. The end product, like a bowl filled with rainbow-colored lettuce leaves, dots of edible flowers and bites of herbs provide a savory finish. ¶ Jill Appenzeller of Appenzeller Landscape Design dug in with stylish salad garden design. Frederique Lavoipierre of Shoestring Nursery, Sebastopol, California; Sky Hoyt, of Lakeport, California; Leonard Diggs of the Farmery, Santa Rosa, California; and Rachel Helm of Buon Gusto Farms, Sebastopol, California, allowed us into their gardens to inspire us with the delicious results of their hard work. We also photographed in the gardens at Mustards Grill, Napa (thanks Rick!), and Stars Oakville, Yountville. Thanks as well to Lisa and Slim, Susan, Forni-Brown-Welch, Beringer Vineyards, Katy Sinnes, the Crow Farmers, and the dedicated gardeners at Green Gulch. ¶ A special thank you to the kind and generous folks in Country Pine English Antiques, Sonoma, for the loan of their charming wheelbarrow for the cover photo. ¶ Mickey Choate and Susan Lescher of The Lescher Agency set up the early framework, like the first survey of the bare garden in earliest spring. My thanks particularly to Hazel White, my editor, whose patient weeding produced a manuscript clean and clear and to Aufuldish and Warinner, our designers, who sort and tidy to fit all the bits and pieces into an organized whole with a stylish clarity that adds poetry to the garden. ¶ To David Carriere, Leslie Jonath, and Bill LeBlond of Chronicle Books, who take over after our work is done, like fine chefs tossing all the ingredients to make a savory whole, we give thanks for continuing our work. ¶ And lastly we thank our families, Bruce LeFavour and Arann and Daniel Harris, the salt and pepper spice of our lives.

The Spanish say that it requires four persons to make a good salad;

A spendthrift for oil, a miser for vinegar, a counsellor for salt, and a madman to stir it up.

From Margaret Huntington Hooker, *Early American Cookery*

❧